CHECK OUT MY "EXTRAS" PAGE WHEN YOU FINISH THE BOOK!

Go to *www.blowthemandown.com/extras* for free access to photos, videos, and audio from my music days. Enjoy the book and THANK YOU for purchasing it!

BLOW THE MAN DOWN

HOW I NAVIGATED THE SAILBOATS AND STATION WAGONS OF THE MUSIC BUSINESS

MARK E. JOHNSON

ISBN# 978-1-7340919-0-8

For anyone who has placed themselves under the glare of a spotlight, behind a live microphone, and tried their best.
You have my respect.

AUTHOR'S NOTE

This is a true story. It is based on my own recollections and those of other people who were there. I will admit, though, that I've used poetic license in places because frankly, my memory of the 1990s is somewhat unreliable, blurry, or even nonexistent here and there. You know the feeling when you're not quite sure if what you recall really happened, or if it was only a dream? It's kind of like that. But there are other people who remember it, too, so I guess it really happened.

Most of the people I've mentioned in this book are — or were — real, but since many of them are still alive and are respectable community citizens with jobs, children, grandchildren, and whatnot, I felt it best that I should change some names, lest I wake up with the severed head of a horse in my bed. In some cases, the individual depicted is a composite of multiple real people, and the timeline is altered in places for my own selfish objectives as an author. I've also changed the names of several other key businesses and a few random things, so if you try to Google them, you may come up empty.

Lastly, I want to say that, despite my mucking around with the details, this is an honest depiction of the life of a blue-collar musician — not a famous pop star. Based on television and movies, you might be led to believe that becoming successful in the entertainment business is no big deal, as simple as being selected for "American Idol" or, if you believed shows like *Nashville*, just showing up in Music City. Within minutes of opening the guitar case — BOOM — you are rich and famous, and rubbing shoulders with Jimmy Fallon and whoever else.

If only that were so. But then, we wouldn't have any good stories, right?

~ Mark E. Johnson, November 13, 2019

PROLOGUE

4:30 pm, Thursday, January 11, 1979

I t was cold. It was really cold. It was the kind of cold that people tell outlandish stories about years later, dropping the temperature even more to make their narrative sound better.

But this weather was so ridiculously frigid, you didn't need to lie about it.

How cold was it? For almost one solid week, the thermometer didn't rise above -18 Fahrenheit. And this wasn't in Alaska or Siberia or somewhere crazy like that. These were the Appalachian Mountains of North Carolina, where things aren't supposed to be that extreme.

We were used to cold winters, but this was a problem. Schools were out, businesses were closed, and events were canceled. Livestock were being sheltered in barns for longer than normal. Outdoor cats and dogs were being brought inside, and there's no telling how many perished.

The cold snap was wreaking havoc on everybody's plumbing across my home county of Ashe, in the very northwest corner of the state. People were bundling up their water pipes as they would their children heading out for a day of sledding. Extension cords were threaded into crawl spaces so electric heaters could be plugged in to provide warmth from below, more often than not unsuccessfully. A few residents, not thinking it through properly, actually built fires under their pipes and promptly burned their homes to the ground.

On my family farm near the foot of Big Phoenix Mountain, the water pipe running between the springhouse and the barn, a distance of roughly 100 yards, had frozen immediately when the temperature plunged, meaning that water must now be carried by hand in 5-gallon buckets to our six horses. My older brother, Greg, had moved out of the house and avoided coming home, even for home-cooked meals, lest he be drafted for a chore like this. My sister, Teri — two years my senior — was sequestered in her bedroom, fretting about teen heartthrob Sean Cassidy and reading Marguerite Henry novels.

As a skinny 13-year-old with little-to-no political influence within the home, the job fell to me.

This day had been the coldest yet: -25 degrees. Night was falling, and the clear sky was becoming bluish-purple, stars already twinkling. In the small stone springhouse, I filled two black plastic buckets and began the interminable journey to the barn. As if I needed even more challenge, 14 inches of new snow blanketed the ground, the crystalline powder filling and leveling every uneven spot and seeming to glow in the lavender dusk. As I walked across the field between the two structures, I repeatedly stepped into divots and dips that I couldn't see, causing me to stumble and slosh water onto my jeans where it froze instantaneously. By the time I reached the barn, the lower parts of my pants were frozen stiff, and my forearms and hands ached.

Six horses meant I had to make three of these trips.

After the third, I huddled in the barn against one of the horses, trying to soak in the body heat of the animal before I had to make my last trek through the deep snow back to the house. The heat generated by Bonnie, Phoenix, Sprite, Sam, Caviar, and Scuttlebutts had raised the temperature of the barn probably a good 10 degrees — in my mind, at least — and I avoided leaving its relative comfort.

It wasn't that I was unaccustomed to harsh environments and hard work. Summers and falls in the tobacco, strawberry, and Christmas tree fields could be brutal. Not only did we endure long days of humid heat and intense sun, but also dealt with snakes, yellow jackets, poison ivy, and even stinging worms that dropped onto our bare arms as we stripped leaves from tall sorghum stalks. Only the occasional afternoon thunderstorm would give us boys an authorized opportunity to goof off and drink iced tea as the booming clouds passed over. But these respites never lasted as long as we hoped.

Late autumn was all about cutting, baling, and loading the heavy conifers onto outbound trucks, destined for big cities like Raleigh and Charlotte. More often than not, we were clad in either yellow rain suits or insulated coveralls, in vain hopes of keeping the rain or snow at bay and would drag ourselves home late at night smelling like a combination of evergreen and diesel fuel.

But January and February were the "off" months, dedicated to repairing farm equipment, cutting, splitting, and stacking firewood, and caring for the horses and chickens.

As I leaned against Bonnie, an elderly quarter horse mare, my mind wandered to my favorite Doc Savage book, *The Man of Bronze*. Doc was probably still down in Central America, shirt ripped to threads and muscles bulging as he raced through Mayan ruins, opening a can of whoop-ass on the bad guys. Whatever he was doing was exotic, awesome, and not watering horses on his dad's Christmas tree farm in sub-zero-degree weather.

Frank and Joe Hardy, my other favorite literary characters,

weren't doing that, either. They were teenaged James Bonds, sneaking around under the moonlight to solve impossible mysteries, going on dates with beautiful damsels, and making the adults look like idiots. Their adventures did not include stinky old rain suits and stupid, boring strawberry plants.

Bonnie snorted in empathy, a cloud of hot breath rising from her nostrils. She shifted slightly as I sprawled across her back.

I thought about our current favorite TV show, *Fantasy Island*. Picturing the swaying palm trees, teal Caribbean water, and scantily clad actresses made me feel a little warmer. Just this afternoon, I had looked up the Caribbean in my parents' World Book Encyclopedia and noticed that the temperature in the U.S. Virgin Islands averaged 75 degrees in January. Can you imagine? Seventy-five degrees! Better yet, there didn't appear to be a Christmas tree in sight.

"Jeez, how does anybody ever get to go to a place like that?" I said aloud, the sound of my pre-pubescent voice making Bonnie turn a lazy brown eye in my direction as she chewed her grain. "It's probably just movie stars and stuff."

For a farm boy on an Arctic winter night in the Blue Ridge Mountains, the warm Caribbean — and any adventure at all — was as distant and inaccessible as the moon itself.

3 pm, Monday, December 6, 1982

We watched in disbelief as President Ronald Reagan strode down the pillared colonnade of the West Wing and into the glass-paneled room, flanked on both sides by Secret Service agents. It wasn't TV; it was real, and he was right there in front of us.

The White House Chief Usher, a man named Rex Scouten, immediately approached the President.

"Mr. President, these are the Johnsons from Ashe County, North Carolina," Scouten said, gesturing to where we were standing. "Mr. and Mrs. Johnson were named 'Grand Champion Growers for 1982' by the National Christmas Tree Association and are providing the White House trees this season."

"Well!" said President Reagan with a broad smile. "Isn't that wonderful? I'm so glad that I could be here to meet you today."

Without hesitation, he walked straight to our family, shaking hands with each one of us individually as the official White House photographer snapped photos. We were all nervous at first, stumbling over our words with quivering voices. My 70-year-old great uncle, a retired truck driver named Owen Walker, was struck mute, unable to utter a single word to the President. Uncle Owen's wife, Aunt Noreen, a rotund, 5-foot-tall fireball, had no problem, though. She never appeared to be intimidated by anything or anyone, even a President, and was rarely at a loss for words. She stepped in front of her petrified husband.

"Oh, don't mind him," she told the Commander-in-Chief and the world's most powerful person with a cackle, grabbing the President's hand with both of hers. "He loves you so much, it's awful!"

The President threw back his head and roared with laughter. For the next 20 minutes, he visited with the Johnsons from North Carolina like old friends.

I watched as my mom and dad spoke easily with President Reagan. Both my parents had grown up in very humble surroundings — Dad, the son of a rural mailman and a house-wife in the foothills of the Appalachians; Mom, the product of a Red Man tobacco-chewing logger and a schoolteacher in North Carolina's coastal plains. Both were salt of the earth but were now realizing a dream beyond dreams.

As we left the White House later, my dad pulled me to one side.

"I want you to remember this day, Mark," Dad said. "Just because you live on a farm in a small town doesn't mean you can't do amazing things in life. You can do anything and go anywhere as long as you want it bad enough and are willing to work for it. Do you understand me, son?"

"Yes, sir," I replied. "I promise I'll remember."

1 pm, Friday, May 14, 1984

"I'm Don Everly, and this is my brother, Phil," I said.

Roughly 600 pairs of confused eyes settled directly on Jerry and me.

I was now a senior at Ashe Central High School, and those eyes belonged to the entire student body.

Jerry and I were clearly not Don and Phil Everly. But there was a good reason why I introduced us that way. At least, it seemed good at the time. Had I known of the mess to which it would eventually lead, I may have reconsidered.

With the end of the school year approaching, the senior drama class had been "working hard" to put together a skit for our fellow students. In reality, this meant that for four months, we had done nothing but tell dirty jokes, draw "Garfield" cartoons in our notebooks, and shoot spitballs at one another in the name of Shakespearean drama.

The day before the event, someone pointed out that the Big Show was tomorrow, and we had prepared absolutely nothing. In a panic, several skits were thrown together, but as an experienced thespian with vast stage experience via the local 4-H drama club, I refused to participate. I had, after all, been cast as the Tin Man in the 4-H Playcrafter's production of *The Wizard of Oz* a few years earlier, and my performance had been singled out in the local newspaper.

"Mark Johnson, 13, played the Tin Man," the article had raved, adding breathlessly that "Johnson carried a wooden ax painted silver as a prop."

(*The Jefferson Times* tended toward flowery commentary.)

So, after such critical success, I wasn't about to ruin my

reputation as a fine stage actor by involving myself with this hack job. Instead, my childhood buddy, Jerry Young, and I devised with a different plan: We would go on stage and entertain the kids with an impersonation of the Everly Brothers.

Having played bluegrass music with my brother since I was 11, I was fairly comfortable performing in front of an audience. (Never mind that the audience usually comprised my somewhat biased parents and whichever aunts and uncles they could round up for an after-dinner concert in the living room.) Jerry was a good singer and had enough natural hutzpah to play along. We both knew three Everly Brothers songs and had sung them together before, just for fun.

Most importantly, though, was the fact that nobody told us we *couldn't* do this. We just decided we would. We were the freaking Hardy Boys.

On performance day, the gymnasium was packed with my school brethren, most of who carried low expectations and were simply excited to be out of class. Although as stage critics, the student body was somewhat forgiving, but my gut feeling about the skit was nonetheless accurate.

It was a train wreck.

Actors were forgetting their lines, had no idea where to stand, and were giggling like skateboarders after a long session in the back of a 1977 conversion van. Mercifully, it ended after about 15 minutes, receiving a smattering of jeers and sarcastic applause.

(For anyone reading this who took part in that play, I give you huge props. Misguided, yes, but it took guts.)

Mrs. Cockerham, the aging drama teacher, then clip-clopped out on her high heels and introduced Jerry and me by our real names, having no idea what we were going to do. Frankly, she had operated in a state of confusion for most of the year — accounting for the lion's share of our ineptitude — but she had tried her best, bless her heart.

Jerry and I were unruffled. We strutted onto the stage with a flourish, me holding the prized Martin D-35 guitar that I had purchased with money I'd earned on the farm. I boldly approached the microphone.

"I don't know who this Mark and Jerry are," I remarked to the audience, which was now as confused as Mrs. Cockerham. "But, I'm Don Everly, and this is my brother, Phil!"

Cough, microphone feedback, the scrape of a metal chair.

"Freebird!" somebody yelled, which created a stir of laughter.

I glanced at "Phil." He gave me a nervous look as if to say, "Go ahead!"

With that, I launched into the opening guitar riff of "Bye, Bye Love." The chunky sound of my Martin D-35 guitar rang gloriously through the gymnasium, bouncing to and fro off the walls. It immediately created a stir, and the kids sat up, clapping their hands in time. Jerry and I crowded the mike like old pros, imitating the Everly's tight, two-part harmony.

The audience erupted in cheers as we finished the first chorus. I shot Jerry an "I believe we're onto something" look as we sang.

Applause growing in intensity with each song, we then played "Walk Right Back" and "Wake Up, Little Susie." As I hit the last chord, the entire student body of Ashe Central High School jumped to its collective feet and — I kid you, not — the screams were deafening. I stood on the stage, flabbergasted, and noticed something.

Most of these screams were coming from girls. Actually, I'd say all of them were.

Now keep in mind, this was 1984, not the 1950s. The top musical artists of the year included Michael Jackson, Huey Lewis, Culture Club, and Van Halen, but Jerry and I had somehow captivated this audience by playing 25-year-old "golden oldie" songs that very few of these kids knew, by artists they'd never heard of, with nothing but vocals and one acoustic guitar. Nonetheless, the girls were responding as I'd hoped, and not just the younger ones. As I scanned the audience, I noticed that some of the best-looking, most popular senior "foxes" were smiling at me in a way they most certainly never had before.

It wasn't that we had suddenly become good-looking; we appeared exactly the same as when we had taken the stage — skinny, awkward, acne-speckled teenagers.

It wasn't because we were all that accomplished; I'm sure we weren't.

It was something else.

At that second, a cartoon light bulb illuminated over my head with an audible "ding." In a moment that would set the course direction for the following two decades of my existence, I had inadvertently but miraculously discovered one of life's greatest inescapable truths. Whether through the mystique of the music itself, our brash confidence, or something yet unknown, the votes were in, and the facts were irrefutable.

Chicks dig musicians.

"Try again. Fail again. Fail better."

SAMUEL BECKETT

1

STATION WAGON

10:30 pm, Tuesday, November 13, 1992

Hunched against a driving rain, I loaded the soft-shell guitar case into the back of my 1979 Dodge Diplomat station wagon, replete with fake wood on the side. Slamming the tailgate shut, I ran to the front and jumped into the driver's seat.

Twenty-three years ago, this was a nice ride, something to be proud of. Now? Not so much. There was a reason I'd parked all the way in the back of the expansive parking lot: I didn't want to be seen in a 1979 Dodge Diplomat station wagon, replete with fake wood on the side.

The car had been given to me by a sympathetic relative, and the odometer was approaching 350,000 miles. As I sat down in the threadbare cloth driver's seat, rain dripping off my nose, I heard a tiny "plink," and something bounced off my knee. Within seconds, the headboard fabric of the car drooped down onto my head.

"Perfect," I said to myself.

I sighed, plucked yet another thumbtack from my ready

supply in the cup holder, and tacked the gauzy fabric back into place. That thumbtack joined approximately 20 others that currently secured the material to the roof, but they would inevitably succumb to gravity and drop onto the seats. Unless I could locate them, the thumbtacks created a sort of minefield for anyone brave enough to sit down in the vehicle.

Although the V-8 engine still ran surprisingly well, the rest of the car was actively falling apart. Only a few of the gauges were operable. The radio still worked, thankfully, but only on AM. The tires were worn slick and had each been patched at least once. Just two days earlier, the entire tailpipe and muffler had dropped off, and now, the station wagon sounded like a vehicle Dale Earnhardt should be driving at Talladega. Hearing me approach from miles away, small-town residents undoubtedly locked their doors and windows, expecting a murderous gang of Hell's Angels bikers. Once, after I had pulled into a gas station, a teenager asked me if I'd customized the car with something called a "cherrybomb glasspack."

I'm not making that up.

"No, but I can tell you how to achieve this sound without paying for a cherrybomb glasspack," I had replied. "Just let your muffler rust off."

"Oh," the boy said, frowning and clearly less impressed with me than he had been earlier. "I guess that would work."

I didn't blame him for his loss of respect. Driving this car, I didn't come off as quirky or artistic or tough. I came off as poor.

Actually, I came off as exactly what I was: an unknown, underfed, 26-year-old bar musician and songwriter. Sure, I complained about the station wagon, but I was thankful to be driving any vehicle that was paid for and would usually get me to the next engagement and meager paycheck.

The car was actually a step up from the 1977 Chevy cargo van that I had been driving until a few months ago. I'd paid $700 for that little rusted-out, army-green beauty.

The van was literally a hornless vehicle. Where the horn had originally been, there was a gaping hole with a large bolt that connected the steering wheel to the steering column. If I wanted to blow my horn at another driver in anger ... well ... I couldn't. I could only gesture at them quietly, which was entirely unsatisfying.

Two years after purchasing the van, I sold it — again for $700 — to a hippie couple who were Renaissance fair enthusiasts. They were practically giddy about the thought of hanging their medieval battle axes and maces from the homemade wooden racks someone had installed in the back years before my ownership. (I'm not making that up, either.)

"The Family Truckster," as I referred to the station wagon in tribute to Clark Griswold's famous vehicle, was the only car left in the parking lot of the Carrboro Arts Center, near Chapel Hill, North Carolina. I grabbed my trusty, dog-eared road almanac to map out my escape back to Interstate 40 but couldn't muster the motivation. I sat at the wheel and stared out the windshield as the nearby streetlight stabbed into the rainy darkness. My breath plumed into the 44-degree air.

I had just completed what should've been my crowning achievement as a musician. I had opened a show for one of my heroes, American folksinger, David Wilcox.

The gig had been arranged by my Nashville publishing company several months earlier as an effort to promote me as a burgeoning folk-rock artist. Every time I heard someone use the word "burgeoning" in reference to me, it made me chuckle. I'd been burgeoning for a long time — more than seven years.

I had recently released my first CD, *Part of Me*, so it did, actually, feel as if things were moving forward with this show. Maybe this was the beginning of the triumphant, rags-to-riches musician story that I could tell Jay Leno or Oprah.

"Mark," Oprah would say to me as the two of us were seated

in comfy chairs on her stage. "Tell us your triumphant, rags-to-riches story."

"Well, Oprah, how much time do you have?" I'd respond, and we'd both laugh like old friends.

But now, as I looked around the car, I could only see rags.

WHEN I ENTERED EAST CAROLINA UNIVERSITY IN THE fall of 1984, I had no designs on becoming a musician. None, whatsoever. I wanted to be a writer.

At some point, though, it dawned on me that the ability to correctly diagram a sentence doesn't tend to inspire hot babes to writhe all over the hood of a car in various stages of undress, like in that Whitesnake video. For any chance at that, I knew that I would need to employ my other half-baked skill: guitar playing.

Within a couple months, I became known among the guys in Garrett Dormitory as "that tall country boy who can play acoustic guitar pretty well and can kind of sing." My room became an informal gathering spot for the guys on my hall, especially for anyone who had a guitar or a harmonica. With the addition of the ringing banjo of Walter, a junior art major who lived a few doors down, the room morphed into an Americana performance venue. Sure, we were closer to the Beverly Hillbillies than Whitesnake, but it was a start.

My roommate, Charles, was a good-natured six-foot-four, 260-pound Haliwa-Saponi Indian who served as the comic relief portion of the program and, if necessary, the bouncer. Between the Evan Williams whiskey and late-night jam sessions, it's a Biblical miracle that we weren't kicked off campus and that any of us passed our freshman year. We had a lot of fun but were still lacking in the Female Companionship Department. Only other *guys* were hearing me play. Not that there's anything wrong with that.

Early in 1985, I hit on an idea: Why not try to learn a few more cover songs and convince some bar or restaurant manager to give me a gig? I could make a few bucks and, most importantly, woo females with my musician-y ways. As a stringbean-ish "nice guy," my particular taxonomy of the male species had at best, limited options for anything beyond dinner and a movie, so I needed an advantage. My dorm-mates were burly, heavily bearded dudes and I was suffering by comparison. Maybe performing music would help level the playing field.

As for the music part, it was just a diversion, an end to a means.

So, I went about the work of becoming a paid singer. I did a little research, identified a target, and armed with some 15 classic folk-rock songs, talked my way into a four-hour gig at St. Andrew's Pub, upstairs at the Beef Barn restaurant in Greenville, North Carolina.

"Sure, I've got a sound system," I lied to the bar manager during my audition. "No problem at all."

"OK, you've got the gig this Friday night," he said. "Be sure you're done by 10 o'clock."

I then drove straight to the nearest phone booth, called my dad, and begged him to front me the money for a sound system. Miraculously, he agreed, and the next day, I purchased a cheap Peavey 4-channel amp, matching speakers, and an inexpensive microphone from the downtown Greenville guitar shop.

Now, I was forced to make a go of it, because I owed Dad just under $600.

St. Andrew's Pub was a small, carpeted bar that had a maximum occupancy of 30. It was wood-paneled and dark, and I could imagine well-to-do old men sitting around the place, smoking pipes, drinking bourbon, and telling war stories. But those guys never attended my shows.

That first night, I had to play each tune four times just to fill the slot, but it didn't matter. The entire audience comprised six of my dorm-mates — the same guys who heard me play every day — and they each quickly became too drunk to notice the repetition. They just thought it was awesome that their friend was playing music in a public venue through a sound system.

"Johnson, you're awesome!" they slurred at me, holding their sloshing beers aloft. "Play another Bunnett ... Buffett!"

These weren't the hot chicks I anticipated, but I soldiered on.

That same week, I landed a part-time job at a small video store, hoping to pay my dad back quickly for the sound equipment. This is only notable because, on my very first day of work, I was assigned the task of alphabetizing and restacking all the pornographic video boxes — hundreds of them — onto the shelves of the "adult" section of the video store, way in the back. In a stroke of incredible benevolence, the store's owner also let me flip on a nearby TV set and watch the ACC basketball tournament as I worked, if you could call it that.

It was the greatest first-day-on-the-job in the history of employment.

The months rolled by, and every week, I would try to learn a couple more songs. Buffett, Taylor, Eagles, Poco, America, Steve Miller Band — you know, that sort of thing. After six months of weekly gigs at the Beef Barn, I could actually do an entire show without playing the same song more than twice, which felt like a victory.

Eventually, I developed a small following that extended beyond only my drunken friends, and that gave me the street cred to book additional engagements at other restaurants. The Beef Barn led to Chico's Mexican Restaurant, which led to a bar called The Fizz, which led to Granddaddy Rosser's Cafe, and so on. Within a year, I was playing three to five times a week and became known as "that guy who knows a bunch of Buffett and James Taylor and can kind of sing." I'm sure there was one of me in every American college town. I just happened to be the one in Greenville, N.C.

Actually, there was more than just me in Greenville. I was the tallest one, though.

My evil scheme of debauchery also began to work. Girls were taking notice, and I was getting dates. Performing music in public was the ultimate method of introduction because I could bypass the awkward "So, do you come here often?" stage. Frankly, all I had to do was play "Don't Let Me Be Lonely Tonight" and allow the chips to fall where they may. For this alone, I owe James Taylor an incredible debt of gratitude.

But something strange was also happening: the idea of becoming a professional musician began creeping in. Maybe this was something I could make a living at. After all, I was staying busy, so I seemed to be doing something right. Days were for attending class, studying for tests, and learning new songs. Nights were for playing music, and with each show, I improved as both a musician and a showman.

The radius of my territory began to expand until it covered most of Eastern North Carolina. I became a gig junkie, a musical prostitute. You have a restaurant with a corner where I can set up? I'll play. You're having a party? I'll play it. Someone died? I'll play at the funeral. (I'm not saying I actually did this, but I certainly would have.) I played bars, steak houses, Mexican restaurants, student coffee houses, sandwich shops, and nightclubs. I played Christmas tree, watermelon, strawberry, and tobacco festivals. I played Holiday Inns, Ramada Inns, and Howard Johnson Inns. I even played for the little old ladies of the Quilters Guild of Greenville at their 8 am meeting in the ballroom of the local Hampton Inn. (The "PA system" they promised to supply turned out to be a speaker podium with the built-in, gooseneck microphone.)

Although these ladies were decidedly above my preferred age bracket, I think I did come away with a couple phone numbers.

If you could gather up a few people and at least pay me in food, I'd play a show for you. For five years, I performed at practically every possible venue in Eastern North Carolina.

Sometimes I fronted a four- or five-piece band with the imaginative name, "MJ & Frenz." I guess by spelling Frenz with a "z," we convinced ourselves it was clever, although I think we were just too embarrassed to give ourselves a proper band name. Real bands, after all, wore crazy clothes, had long hair, and stayed stoned on hard drugs. When off stage, they laid around the band house in a haze of marijuana smoke.

We, on the other hand, were just average college guys and respectable men with real jobs. We weren't worthy of a cool moniker. Plus, we hardly ever rehearsed and our setlist was made up of songs that we all just happened to know. We usually sounded pretty good once the song got going, but beginnings and ends were often sloppy, cringe-worthy affairs.

Nonetheless, people seemed to like us.

Including myself, the group consisted of Luke Whisnant, my freshman English composition professor at ECU who became my buddy and lead guitarist; bass player Ronnie Daw, who managed the guitar shop where I bought my PA system; drummer Stan Simmons, an ECU cheerleader and construction management major; and, on occasion, Michael Robertson, a music student who played Latin percussion and with his big set of congas, made us appear more impressive on stage than we actually sounded, I suspect.

Often, Luke and I played as a duo. That band name was even more inspired: "Mark Johnson with special guest, Luke Whisnant."

We missed the opportunity to go with "MJ and *Fren*."

During one 10-day stretch, Luke and I played so many consecutive shows that by the end of it, we were literally falling asleep at our microphones or would become slaphappy and start giggling uncontrollably like fools, leaving the audience confused. At one venue, this began literally with the opening note of the first song when my overtaxed voice cracked right out of the box, sending both of us into an irreversible spasm of giggles. Each time one would pull it together, the other would snicker and the whole thing would fall apart again. It must've lasted at least five minutes.

"Is this part of the show?" I heard an elderly lady seated near the stage ask her husband. "I much prefer Gleason."

One way or another — whether in the band or as a solo act — I was playing music to the exclusion of almost everything else. This would last from 1985 to 1990.

Sounds good, right? In many ways, yes, but it was similar to Kevin Costner's character, Crash Davis, breaking the Minor League home run record in the movie, *Bull Durham*. As he pointed out, the record was a "dubious honor," and he didn't really want that kind of notoriety. This made perfect sense to me. Either I moved up to The Show — a career recording and performing original music — or I would end up as a sad, creepy, middle-aged guy with a mullet playing "You've Got a Friend" to 18-year-old sorority sisters, swaying arm-in-arm and singing in unison in a single monotone drone.

I promised myself never to become *that* guy.

So I resolved to change course. I began to shift my focus from learning cover songs to writing originals. At first, I was terrified, frozen by the fear of inadvertently plagiarizing other known songs, and then being called out as a cheat or, worse yet, unoriginal. It took me six months to work up the courage to play my first original composition, "Trouble Keeping Good Times," in public. When I did, I played it without an introduction at all, just to get an authentic reaction.

Predictably, the audience response was to drink more beer, eat more tortilla chips and salsa, and continue their conversations without pause.

I was annoyed but undeterred and kept writing and mixing in my own material whenever I felt that I could get away with it. Sometimes, if the response was positive, I would reveal to the audience that it was my own song. Most times, I didn't. Regardless, I sensed that I had at least a modicum of ability, and this was what I should be doing.

It wasn't even up for debate.

Sometime in 1988, I purchased a Fostex 4-track recorder, set up a tiny studio in the corner of my apartment bedroom, and began recording myself. Whatever time had been devoted to studying for school during the day was now diverted to recording, and I became a hermit, hunched over my Fostex like a mad scientist for days on end. I practiced singing harmony by recording all the vocal parts to songs like Crosby, Stills & Nash's "Suite: Judy Blue Eyes" and James Taylor's "Traffic Jam." Inspired by jazz artist Bobby McFerrin, I would sing bass parts and play percussion by slapping my knees or chest. I'm quite certain that 99.99 percent of this was unlistenable garbage, but it didn't matter. I was young, enthusiastic, and learning.

By the end of the year, I had recorded enough original music to make a full "album" of sorts. I used a dual cassette deck to dub tapes one at a time and began selling them at my shows for $5 each. The name of the collection, appropriately, was *Homemade*. I sketched the cover art, and Luke created the liner notes on his Macintosh computer, the first one I had ever seen in person.

By September of 1990, I was fully invested in the musician life. Even though I had squeaked by with enough decent grades to earn my English degree, I couldn't imagine myself doing anything but music, so within days of receiving my diploma, my North Carolina residency ended. I loaded a U-Haul trailer, hooked it to a borrowed pickup truck, and pointed the rig west, directly at Nashville, Tennessee. I didn't know a soul in Music City and had no idea what I was doing, but at 24, anything seemed possible.

If I were going to do this, there was no time like the present.

2

CITY OF DREAMS

Nashville was vast and frightening. Confusing, one-way streets crisscrossed the city, often changing names without warning, and three major interstate highways collided near downtown, creating a crush of traffic. The town was full of nondescript, boxy, concrete skyscrapers that all appeared to have been built in the 1960s and '70s — long, rectangular boxes tipped onto one end. Even on sunny days, the town seemed gray, dreary, and dirty, as if it was designed to quell the explosive creativity of the thousands of musicians and songwriters who had migrated there.

"Stay down, you creative sons of bitches!" Nashville shouted at us, planting a grubby boot on our foreheads. "I'll decide who succeeds around here! Talent has nothing to do with it!"

During the day, Lower Broadway, the main tourist section of downtown, was often packed with country music enthusiasts visiting the honky-tonks and record stores.

They were all dressed like John Travolta in *Urban Cowboy*.

This confused me then and still does. Why would anyone choose to wear a cowboy hat and boots to walk around an urban metropolis? It was akin to wearing full pads and a helmet to watch a football game.

By night, especially after 10 or 11 pm, Lower Broad, as it's known, became a haven for prostitutes, drug dealers, and various other low-lives, including us musicians. If you were a longhair like me, you could generally blend in reasonably well and move about freely, but even then, you had to keep your head on a swivel.

I had acclimated to Nashville with surprising ease. Through a third-party contact, I had found a guy — even before I left North Carolina — who needed a roommate, so housing was taken care of. The West Nashville apartment was old and worn, but livable. The roommate, a total stranger to me, was an irascible air-conditioner salesman with whom I had little in common, but we stayed out of each other's way.

Within two weeks of arriving, I took a job at a local lawn and garden center, lugging bags of fertilizer and watering nursery stock. Each evening, I'd shower up and either work on whatever song I was writing at the time or attend a writers-in-the-round show at the famous Bluebird Cafe or some other venue.

Finding work as a musician was practically impossible unless that person was willing to play for free or, possibly, for food. Instead of working at their craft, musicians made ends meet as waiters, bartenders, telemarketers, construction workers, receptionists, dishwashers, and fertilizer luggers like me. It was all very glamorous, just like the TV shows.

A single job was rarely enough. On days that I wasn't needed at the nursery, I worked as a commissioned salesman for a door-to-door frozen meat company.

Yes, you read that correctly.

I would drive my duly assigned white Ford Ranger pickup truck with a freezer strapped down in the back into random Nashville neighborhoods. Choosing houses based on their perceived lack of a vicious dog, I would approach, ring the doorbell, and try to convince the aghast resident to purchase boxes of "flash-frozen" ribeyes, Delmonicos, and fillets out of my freezer.

"Good morning, ma'am. I'm Mark Johnson with Insane Frozen Meat Company (not the real name). I'm here in your neighborhood making deliveries (that's a lie) and noticed your address hasn't been added to my regular route (bullshit line to make it sound real). Would you be interested in checking out my quality (wretched) beef, pork, and chicken products?"

You can imagine how well this went over. I may have sold one pork chop.

For another block of time, I again worked as a door-to-door salesman, this time for a vinyl siding company.

(And yes, your assumption is correct: any idiot could get a door-to-door sales job.)

Along with three other equally pathetic losers, I would climb into the back seat of a claustrophobic 4-door sedan owned by my "manager," and he would drive to the most destitute neighborhood possible where we would "canvas," the Latin origin of which means either "made of hemp" or " to walk around horrible neighborhoods and purposely annoy people who have weapons and vicious, snarling dogs."

On my first day with that company — and I'm not kidding — we watched as a man was gunned down in the street. The reaction of the manager was to calmly steer the vehicle into the adjacent neighborhood to do our canvassing. It was one of those weird moments where life imitates art, if art is *Law & Order*.

Every day thereafter that someone wasn't gunned down I viewed as an improvement.

After first determining that I wasn't about to be murdered, my usual spiel went like this.

"Good morning, sir. I'm Mark Johnson with Insane Vinyl Siding Company (might as well have been called that). I'm here in your neighborhood on a service call (another lie) and noticed that your soffits and gutters seem to be slightly worn (falling apart like the rest of the house). Would you be interested in a free estimate for replacing your home coverings and accessories (termite-infested, meth-infused wood that I can clearly see through)?"

This went over almost as well as the frozen meat routine.

What made this job even better was the fact that on many shifts, the manager would decide that it was more productive if he parked the car at the end of a sketchy street and we all sat there smoking cigarettes and telling raunchy jokes for two hours before calling it a day. As a non-smoker, I enjoyed this activity immensely and would often feign falling asleep with my nose next to the cracked window. This served as a defense mechanism to dying of asphyxiation or having my sense of smell permanently damaged by an atmosphere of cigarette smoke and body odor.

Again, "glamour" is the word I would use.

These jobs all had an interesting effect on my psyche. They generally filled me with hope, confidence, and pride in myself for making it home without gunshot wounds or being mauled by an animal each day. Where, in most cases, a successful day on the job involves earning money, I viewed survival as a victory. In all honesty, though, having been raised on a farm had made me impervious to nearly any horrendous line of work. I knew that if I could make it through those 90-degree summers in the Christmas tree and tobacco fields, I could handle almost anything.

Plus, I was here on a mission.

By 1991, I had created a substantial catalog of original material and one day, another friend of a friend introduced me to a well-known publisher on Music Row, a former record executive we'll call Reggie Hamm for the purposes of this book. Almost miraculously, I landed a staff writer position with the guy.

My monthly advance was almost enough to pay the rent but

fell short for other luxuries, like food. Determining that the door-to-door jobs were costing more in transportation than I was actually making, I began to travel and play cover gigs. Missouri, Texas, Kentucky, California, Georgia...wherever I could get booked.

When in Nashville, the crap day jobs continued. I worked as a dishwasher at an Applebee's restaurant, a warehouse laborer, a document scanner, a paper-clip remover (not kidding), and anything else a local temp agency needed me to do. I wrote song after song for the publishing company and recorded demos between day jobs. For an entire year, my primary source of sustenance was the 85-year-old lady, Ms. Bea, who lived in the apartment next door and insisted I share her dinner almost every night. Her ancient Tupperware bowls smelled like mothballs, and the food was usually freezer-burned, but I was glad to have it.

"You take this chicken tetrazzini and warm it up," Ms. Bea would say. "Just scrape off that top layer of ice. It's been in the freezer a little while."

The phrase "a little while" roughly equated to "since the Carter administration." Sometimes I could eat the food, sometimes I couldn't, but in every case, I made sure that she believed I did.

In the spring of 1992, Reggie decided we'd put together a collection of my demos, polish them up a bit, and release a CD in hopes of getting me signed to a major label as an artist. One day, Reggie called me.

"You available to be in Chapel Hill on November 13?" he asked.

"I guess. Why?"

"You're opening for David Wilcox."

3

FRUIT TRAY

I t was new territory. The concept of opening a show for an established artist in a real theater with a paying audience was...well...mind-blowing. I was horrified that someone would out me as the same guy who used to play cover tunes at the Beef Barn, exposing me for the imposter I was.

But I had to continue with the ruse.

The hours leading up to the show were somewhat dreamlike. I met David, his wife, and the couple's new baby at the 3 pm soundcheck. It was just the four of us plus the sound guy in the darkened, 355-seat Wynn Theater.

I had tried to be cool when I introduced myself to David but probably failed miserably. According to established laws of nature, it's impossible to act normal in the presence of your heroes, and I was no exception.

Me: Hi, I'm... uh ... uh ...

David: Oh, you must be Mark. Hi, I'm David.

Me: Yes, hello, Mark. I'm David.

At the time, David was signed to a major label, A&M Records, and was viewed as the next folk musician who might transition into the pop world and become a major commercial success, similar to James Taylor's breakthrough in 1970. I even covered several of David's songs in my show.

Despite my awkwardness and apparent confusion over my own name, the Wilcoxes were warm, friendly, and personable. Predictably, when it came my turn to play through the sound system, I was mortified to be performing in front of David. I nonetheless used one of my more complex songs for the sound-check. As I played, David walked onto the stage and stood directly in front of me, peering at my left hand.

"Are you in standard tuning?" he demanded over my singing.

As you can imagine, I was entirely unnerved by this and stopped playing.

"Um, yep. Standard tuning."

"Wow," David replied. "Cool."

It was a big compliment for me, because David was renowned as one of the industry's most innovative and talented guitar players and was known particularly for playing in alternate tunings. My hands were shaking as I returned my guitar to its case.

And then, it was almost showtime.

Backstage, the minutes ticked by much faster than normal. I was nervous but nonetheless reveled in the experience. Usually before a show, I was waiting in The Family Truckster or sitting at a bar. The last time I had experienced a proper backstage was when I played the Tin Man in 7th grade, so this was heady stuff. There was even a small table set out with a snack tray of fruit and cheese.

This is The Show! I told myself.

David and I chatted about family and music and tuned our guitars obsessively. I could tell by the sound of the murmuring crowd on the other side of the closed curtain that the place was packed. My heart thudded in my chest.

Suddenly, it was 7 pm, and I heard the house music go away.

The emcee approached the microphone and welcomed the crowd.

"Good evening, ladies and gentlemen, and welcome to the Carrboro Arts Center..."

Here we go. I tried desperately to calm my quivering knees.

The guy then introduced me, and I entered the stage to a polite round of applause, slightly more than a smattering. These were, after all, folk-music fans in the Deep South, so I expected good manners and they reacted accordingly.

"Howdy, y'all," I said into the mic. "I'm Mark Johnson, and I'm sure honored to be opening for David. Thank you for being here tonight."

I then began my first song, a Little Feat-inspired number called "Calypso Café," which I had co-written with my friend, Dennis Ritchie[1]. As the booming sound of my recently purchased Takamine guitar rang through the amplifiers, I was immediately at ease.

I knew how to do this, and I knew it was good.

Whatever nervous quiver had been in my voice disappeared, and I sang with strength and in tune. My fingers felt perfect on the metal, light-gauge strings, and the words of the song rolled past my mind's eye as if on a teleprompter. Even against the glare of the stage lights, I could make out the audience, and their eyes were locked on mine, heads bobbing in time. The song finished in a quiet fade to nothing, and there was a moment of silence before the audience erupted into raucous applause.

This is fun, I thought. More fun, even, than the Beef Barn.

For 20 minutes, I played my best tunes and ended with the song, "Above the Sound," which was inspired by a Stephen Coonts novel and told the tragic story of a doomed Naval aviator.

I am dead on the ground/As I wait for my turn

33

I hope for afterlife/God knows I count on afterburn
I am swallowed up in darkness/No longer earthbound
I can't hear you anymore/I am flying above the sound

I had written the song as an exercise, attempting to place myself into an entirely foreign-to-me situation — that of a fighter pilot in his F/A-18 Hornet. I wanted to address the universal song themes of love, loss, and struggle in an entirely unexpected and unusual way. It turned out to be one of my best.

The tune climaxed in an eclectic power chord that shook the walls of the theater, mainly because I shoved the gain control of my acoustic/electric guitar up to the max as the song concluded. The audience leaped to its collective feet and cheered.

I had done it. I hadn't embarrassed myself and had even created some possible new fans. As far as I could tell, none of these people were drunk or stoned, either.

Things would be different now.

As I waved and walked off the stage, the audience thundered, actually stomping for an encore, which of course, I didn't oblige. But it was tempting.

In the darkened backstage, I passed David heading in the other direction.

"Nice job," he said quietly without smiling or slowing down. "You really got them going."

Based on our previous interactions, this seemed oddly unenthusiastic to me, but I brushed it off. He was focused on his show and rightly so.

David was met with a loud cheer from the crowd. Regardless of what I had done, this was clearly his audience. He played the first song without any type of introduction and then spoke to the room.

"I want to start by thanking you for coming," he said. "I'd also like to thank the Carrboro Arts Center for having me. Isn't this venue great?"

Applause.

This is where he's going to mention me, I said to myself, listening through the curtain. This is where I'll finally be legitimized by a real artist in front of God and everyone. This will be my jumping-off point. Maybe I'll even start touring with David! No, that's crazy. At the very least, he will comment on the hungry young songwriter who worked his audience into a frenzy.

Nothing. David launched into his second tune without acknowledging me in any way. Another song passed, then another.

I was dumbfounded. Any time I had seen a popular act that included an opener, the star had thanked the first band or musician, even if they had sucked. I'm pretty sure that I hadn't sucked at all, but by this point in the show, it would've been strange to mention me to the audience.

Was he mad at me for playing my songs well? Could that be possible? Why would he agree to an opening act that was an embarrassment to his audience?

I walked out into the back of the theater and watched the rest of his show from the shadows. David finished his last song, shook some hands, and disappeared. After that, I never saw him again. He and his family must have left through the backstage exit.

In a matter of two hours, I had been raised to an unthinkable height, only to be dropped immediately back to Earth. It wasn't a gentle landing, either. The chutes never opened.

As the lights came up and the crowd dispersed, I began slinking back toward the backstage door, hoping nobody would see me, but sure enough, an older lady stopped me.

"We loved you too, Mike," she said, patting my shoulder. "Keep at it. One day maybe you can make a record like David!"

"Yes, ma'am, thank you," I said without correcting her. "Watch for me in the records stores. Mike Johnson."

Backstage, I packed up my guitar in a daze, my mind trying to process what had just happened, struggling with the correct response. Just before heading out the door, I sidled back and emptied the cheese platter into the pockets of my jacket.

"Screw 'em if they think I'm leaving this," I whispered to myself, grabbing a handful of napkins.

It would be a long return trip to Nashville, but I had to get back. After all, those ribeyes and Delmonicos weren't going to sell themselves.

---

1. Dennis was also an accomplished sound engineer who had recorded all of my stuff and dozens of classic country albums.

4

GAS MONEY

In many ways, the Wilcox experience was a valuable learning moment. I realized, over time, that David had done nothing wrong. He had just neglected to go out of his way to promote another musician, which was certainly not his job. It began to dawn on me that professional music was not populated with friendly people who inexplicably felt the need to assist me simply because I was nice and used good manners. The music business was just that — a business. An insanely competitive one.

I was learning to manage, if not lower my expectations, and to proceed with a new degree of cynicism. Like a pro football team winning a playoff game, the enjoyment of a victory in the music business was a fleeting thing. It could be relished only for a moment because another challenge was around the next corner, usually with an equally jarring helping of disappointment.

I tried to forget the whole thing. The next six months were filled with travel throughout the Southeast U.S. to $50-100-per-night engagements, writing new songs, and, of course, simple survival.

Every day in Nashville was a strange contradiction. Either I was a nobody toiling at the lowest rung of the socioeconomic ladder, or I was bumping shoulders with famous musicians at lavish industry parties, clubs, or in the Music Row building where my publishing company was headquartered. Even though I was an unknown, it seemed that the younger, current stars often treated me with mutual respect because (I'm theorizing here) they assumed I was somebody they *should* know. It was an underlying political vibe that made me uneasy, although most of these people were perfectly nice.

I didn't get this vibe from the older country music stars. They were usually just straight-up friendly. I met Grandpa Jones and "Whispering" Bill Anderson backstage at the Grand Ole Opry one night, and they seemed genuinely pleased to meet me, too. Another time in a recording studio, I hung out with The Jordanaires, the legendary background singers who recorded a zillion hits with Elvis Presley, Patsy Cline, and many others. I sat quietly in amazement as they discussed recording the background vocals to Elvis' "Blue Christmas," laughing about how unofficial member Millie Kirkham thought the distinctive high soprano part was silly and had a hard time taking it seriously.

Occasionally, one of my heroes turned out better than I could've imagined. Take Sonny Curtis, for example. I was stunned, one evening at a party, to be introduced to Sonny, a legend among musicians. Sonny had been a member of Buddy Holly's band, The Crickets, and was the writer of classic songs like "I Fought the Law and the Law Won," "I'm No Stranger to the Rain," and the theme of *The Mary Tyler Moore Show*, which he also sang. What made him personally important to me is that he wrote The Everly Brothers' hit "Walk Right Back," one of the three songs I sang with Jerry Young that day in high school.

There seemed to be no ego in Sonny at all, and he greeted me like a peer, putting me at ease. As we stood in a kitchen holding cups of iced tea, I recounted the story of performing his song, and how that had led me into the industry. Sonny was thrilled, and we spent the better part of the evening hanging out and talking music. I made a mental note that if I ever became someone's hero, I would conduct myself like Sonny Curtis.

Another night, I was with my good friend and fellow North Carolina musician, Bruce Frye, at the Bluebird Cafe when Jon Bon Jovi strolled in with his entourage. Next thing I knew, we were sipping beers with Bon Jovi, an amiable guy. (Bruce had an impressive knack of getting through the "gate-keepers" to hang out with celebrities.) Bon Jovi and I ran into each other again at another club later that night. This time, he was alone, and seemed relieved to see a familiar face. We hung out at the bar for a little while until he was spotted and overrun by fans, shoving their way past me to get between us. He gave me an apologetic shrug as I ducked out.

I slunk back home to my freezer-burned Ms. Bea meal.

Then there was the Mother-Of-All-Foot-In-Mouth-Incidents, also at the Bluebird. On a nondescript Tuesday evening, I spent nearly an hour in the back of the club, chatting with a friendly patron who identified himself as "just another songwriter." The man was, I estimated, in his 40s, with a gaunt frame and stringy black hair combed back from a lined face. In my Appalachian vernacular, he looked rode hard and put up wet. I wondered if he might be homeless.

Emboldened by several beers, I bragged about how many times I'd played the Bluebird and how I had landed a staff writing position on Music Row.

"Good luck with your songwriting!" I encouraged the man with a Barney Fife sniff. "Keep working at it. You'll get there!"

It wasn't until he was leaving that we introduced each other. He held out a bony hand.

"I'm Townes Van Zandt," he said with a knowing smile. "It's been nice to meet you."

My heart dropped into my feet.

"I'm Mark Johnson," I replied. "Now if you'll excuse me, I'll go fling myself off the nearest bridge."

I'd been blustering about myself to one of the most renowned, beloved songwriters in country music history without recognizing him, the guy who had composed such classics as "Pancho and Lefty," and "If I Needed You." After nearly 30 years, it still makes me cringe.

SOME DAYS, MY WORLD OF CELEBRITY ENCOUNTERS tilted into absurd surrealism. On a frigid January afternoon, the Family Truckster became stuck in the middle of a Music Row intersection during an ice storm. I could go neither forward nor back for two full cycles of the traffic light, and rust flew in every direction as my treadless tires spun wildly back and forth on the icy pavement, clouds of smoke billowing out of the hole where the muffler used to be.

To make matters worse, the heater in the Truckster had recently died, so I had to drive around Nashville dressed like I was embarking on an Arctic expedition, topped off by a very uncool toboggan with the puffy ball on top.

As I desperately tried to move the car out of the intersection, a sleek, black $50,000 Range Rover pulled slowly around me. In the driver's seat — much to my amazement — was the chart-topping, universally loved, and impossibly handsome country singer, Billy Dean. He was mostly known for his heart-breaking love ballad, "Somewhere in My Broken Heart." He slowed the massive SUV to a crawl.

Oh, thank God, I thought to myself. *Billy Dean is going to stop and help me push this thing out of the way.*

Instead, the singer laid on his horn, shouted obscenities, and glared at me through the closed window of his luxury vehicle. The windows were so well insulated that I could barely make out his muffled, enraged voice. (Although clearly angry, he looked really warm and comfortable in there, of which I was jealous.)

Even after all I had already been through, this was more than I could handle, and I exploded.

"Fuck you, Billy Dean!" I shrieked, shooting him double birds with both arms out my open window. "You've got a big ass and your songs suck!"

(OK, it was all I could think of in the heat of battle.)

Billy Dean's eyes widened, and he sped away, clearly terrified. A few years later, the singer was actually in my audience as I played a Bluebird Cafe show. I resisted the urge to leap off the stage and pummel him about the head and shoulders with my guitar, mainly because I actually liked his music and I could only afford one guitar.

NASHVILLE IN THE EARLY '90S WAS EXPLODING. IN A smooth exchange, Garth Brooks, Alan Jackson, and Clint Black had taken the baton from Randy Travis, who had single-handedly resuscitated traditional country music in the late 1980s. Garth had made it mainstream, a spectacle, and now, the genre was threatening pop as the music to consume. No longer was country only for your grandpa and the camouflage crew living out in the sticks, drinking moonshine.

Songwriters of all genres smelled opportunity and migrated to the city; even acoustic rock guys like me. Nashville was churning out contemporary Christian, rap, metal, and even world music in addition to standard country, and almost everybody viewed the place as vastly more livable than either Los Angeles or New York, the two other entertainment centers.

I was somewhere slightly ahead of most in the game — I had a publisher and was playing writer shows — but was on the lowest tier of the "professional songwriter" designation, joined by countless others. The city was thick with talented and experienced singers and guitarists. It seemed that every other person I met identified himself or herself as a songwriter, just as Los Angeles is full of actors. Success in the Nashville music industry was a nearly impenetrable egg with gazillions of musician sperm swimming furiously and competing to be the chosen one. Just when you thought you might wriggle through, some other little bastard beat you to the punch.

Every day I awoke to an insane range of possibility that was both exciting and terrifying. Today could be the day I would be offered a major-label recording contract, for example, or receive a phone call that Garth had recorded one of my songs and the hard times were over. It could also be the day I would be evicted from my musty apartment for non-payment.

Either was possible, although the latter was much more likely.

I would drive my junk vehicle to demo recording sessions, spend the afternoon singing and playing guitar into microphones worth more than the Truckster with famous, A-string musicians and producers, and then have to sell my beloved softball glove to a used sporting-goods store for enough gas money to get me home.

This is true. I sold a $125 Wilson softball glove for $15 worth of gas, one of my few regrets in life.

At night, if I didn't have a Ms. Bea meal, I ate spaghetti noodles with chicken broth poured over them just to break up the monotony of peanut butter sandwiches.

I lived simply. The only belongings in my apartment were a bed and dresser, a cheap Sears stereo system, an ancient television, and a plastic folding lounge chair that served as my living room furniture. If anybody visited, I'd give them the chair, and I sat on the floor.

I applied for the dishwashing job at Applebee's because it

was within walking distance of my Berry Hill apartment. When I interviewed for the position, the young manager looked at my resume and then back at me, his eyes narrowing.

"You've got a college degree," he said. "Why do you want this job?"

"I just need something to keep me alive and give me enough time to write music," I said. "I promise I'll be the best dishwasher you've ever had, though."

And I was. I was also the only guy in the kitchen who was not on parole.

So, what did I do with my oversized, college-educated brain? As the guy also responsible for preparing desserts every morning, I devised a way to produce nine slices of cheesecake when there should've only been eight. I would hide the ill-gotten slice somewhere in the kitchen where I could eat it when no one was looking.

While juggling these two realities, the dirty side of the big-time music business began to reveal itself. I had written and demoed a song called "Join the Club" in 1992 and had been playing it at writer's shows around Nashville. In '93, a young Tim McGraw released a single called "Welcome to the Club" which was very, very similar in content. Several of the session musicians who had played on my demo had also participated on McGraw's album, so the appearance of the song seemed beyond coincidental. One of my fellow songwriters called me one day.

"I just heard 'Join the Club' on the radio," he said, making my heart leap into my throat. "Only it's called something else and the music is different."

This would happen to me again in 1995. I had co-written the song, "On the Front Porch," with a lovely young lady named Cyndi Torres. Without warning, our song appeared on the radio as the slightly altered "If the World Had a Front Porch," and zoomed up the country charts to #2 for singer Tracy Lawrence. He had recorded the hit only a couple months after our version, and the demo singer of both "On the Front Porch" *and* "Join the Club" turned out to be one of the co-writers of the Lawrence song. It wasn't difficult to connect the dots.

That was a gut punch I would never fully recover from.

IT WAS SPRING 1994 AND MY CD, "PART OF ME," WAS accomplishing nothing more than helping me get an occasional gig. Several of the songs had been put "on hold" by various established artists, which is another way of saying "I'm probably not going to record this song, but I don't want anyone else to record it either until I take roughly a millennium to make a decision, which will almost definitely be no." Though it sounded impressive to the folks back home to say, "Alan Jackson has one of my songs on hold," I knew that it was meaningless.

It was better, I guess, than saying "Alan Jackson *doesn't* have one of my songs on hold."

A few of my songs had been cut by local indie bands — one with the unlikely name of "Fish Heads and Rice" — but the bottom line was, I just wasn't marketable. My material wasn't formulaic enough for Nashville, wasn't edgy enough for grunge-obsessed Los Angeles, and I wasn't believable as either a country or rock singer.

I didn't fit anywhere.

I was a better-than-average guitar player, but couldn't read music or the Nashville Number System (a method of transcribing music based on chords rather than single notes), so I had no future as a session player.

To make matters worse, Reggie had rubbed too many people the wrong way over his years in the music industry and was, for all practical purposes, blacklisted. Even if my songs had been perfect, the people who really mattered weren't hearing them. If they were, those people more than likely held grudges against Reggie and weren't about to record anything from his catalog.

During this strange period, I met a rangy blonde songwriter named Ellen through mutual friends, and we embarked on a brief but torrid relationship. I was always amazed that any attractive woman would remain interested in me after seeing my pitiful apartment and The Family Truckster, but I soon realized that they were probably dating me for my "potential" more than anything else. It certainly wasn't for the money.

Maybe it was for the hair. I had good hair.

Anyway, Ellen was also a seasoned performer and had contacts among club owners across the country. We spent a lot of time comparing notes and trading performance stories. One day that spring, she told me about a friend who had recently played a long-term engagement on the U.S. Virgin Island of St. Croix, a place I'd only heard of in passing.

"You should do that," she told me, poking me in the shoulder with her finger as we reclined in her funky, hipster apartment, complete with burning incense and Asian tapestries. "You know all the right kind of songs. They would love you. And I've got the phone number of the guy who owns the club."

At first, the idea seemed so outrageous, I hardly entertained it. That kind of job was reserved for others — actual entertainers — not me. Although I'd traveled quite a bit within the continental U.S., I'd never been out of the country and was, at heart, still a small town, North Carolina mountain boy, not an adventurer. Sure, I'd played hundreds, perhaps thousands, of gigs over eight years, but I still couldn't shake the feeling that I was an imposter who was only pretending to be a musician. At some point, they would find me out.

Despite these misgivings, the idea lingered in my subconscious.

The sun, the water... the girls.

Like many people, I'd always been fascinated by the

Caribbean. According to TV, people arrived there by seaplane, wore gauzy white shirts and pants, and didn't seem to have a care in the world, which was the exact opposite of what I was currently experiencing.

After letting the concept simmer for a week or two, I asked Ellen for the phone number. One afternoon after my Applebee's dishwashing shift ended, I dialed it, and after a few rings, a male voice answered.

"Soggy Beard Adventures. May I help you?"

"Yes, may I speak to Ernest Alvarez, please?"

"Speaking."

"Hi, Ernest. This is Mark Johnson. I'm a musician in Nashville, Tennessee, and was referred to you by a friend who knows one of your past acts. Do you have a second to talk?"

This began a series of back and forth phone calls that climaxed two weeks later, after Ernest had received and listened to my CD. He called and offered me a two-month gig at his bar — The Mizzenmast — starting in January 1995, some five months later. There wasn't much money in it, Ernest had said, but he would put me up in a small apartment above the bar. Thanking him, I told him I'd "check my schedule" and call him back.

I hung up the phone, immediately embarrassed that I'd said such a stupid thing, and stood quietly in my apartment, the only sound being the ticking of the wall clock I'd bought at Dollar General for $4. My brain was racing through the variables of what had just been presented to me.

If I left Nashville for two months, that might be just the break the next guy needed. There was no guarantee that I could keep my entry-level publishing deal even when I was in town. Sure, the Caribbean represented three steady meals per day, but also a complete and utter unknown, as foreign to a guy like me as Europe or Asia. I had no idea what to expect, or what I would do there, aside from playing cover songs.

I made a quick inventory. The front of my jeans was covered in a disgusting wet paste of uneaten food, grease, and detergent from the Applebee's kitchen. Within my field of view were a guitar, a jumble of notebook paper scribbled with lyrics spilling off a folding lawn chair inside perhaps the worst apartment in Nashville, and white plaster walls.

I was 27 years old and had a whopping $14 in my bank account.

I currently had a song on the country charts, but my name wasn't on the credits, I wasn't getting paid for it, and if I said anything about it, people would think I was an asshole, a con artist, or both.

All that was in my kitchen was a container of spaghetti noodles, freezer-burned chicken tetrazzini, and a box of Lucky Charms cereal.

I was going nowhere and contributing to nothing.

"The hell with all of this," I said out loud to nobody and everybody. "I'm going to St. Croix."

I picked up the phone and pushed "redial."

5

RHONDA'S TRUCK

T he wheels of my American Airlines "puddle jumper" touched down at St. Croix's tiny Henry E. Rohlsen Airport on Tuesday, January 3, 1995. It was around dusk, and as I descended the steps to the tarmac, I noted that the air was damp, warm, and ... well ... different.

That made it perfect.

I arrived in St. Croix woefully under-informed. I knew I was playing six nights a week, my hours were 9 p.m. to 2 a.m., I'd make $50 per gig, and I started tomorrow. That was about it. I had convinced Ernest Alvarez to front me his half of the airfare because I couldn't manage to raise the dough without selling my guitar, and I'm pretty sure The Mizzenmast wasn't looking for an a cappella act. I knew that if I could just get to the island and start playing, I could survive. I arrived with $50 in my pocket.

Of island life, I was clueless. By now, the Internet did exist, but I had no idea how to use it, let alone find information about St. Croix. There was no YouTube where I could watch videos. I couldn't afford a book about St. Croix, and it never occurred to me to check one out of a library. All I really knew was that I needed warm-weather clothing and my guitar. In fact, when I left Nashville, it was 21 degrees Fahrenheit and snowing, yet I walked into the airport wearing nothing but a t-shirt and jeans, which I'm sure raised some eyebrows.

Six hours later, here I was.

The baggage claim area of the airport was an open-air pavilion with a small conveyor belt struggling to move the luggage around the circle, old metallic gears whining in protest. I had caught my first sample of the distinctive Caribbean dialect on the plane, which was filled mostly with native islanders returning home from Puerto Rico. Now, they were chattering away as we waited for our bags. I was surrounded by coal-dark people in vibrant, colorful dress speaking a language I was pretty sure was English — I just couldn't quite make out what they were saying. Most of them were shooting glances at me. As a six-foot, five-inch white guy with hair halfway down my back and a guitar case in one hand, I was the proverbial sore thumb.

"You must be Mark," came an American-sounding voice from behind me. I turned to see a smiling, sunburned face peering out from a mane of out-of-control, bleached-blond hair. The young woman introduced herself as Rhonda Shanks, manager of The Mizzenmast. Ernest had dispatched her to pick me up.

"Welcome to the island," she said with a wide, attractive grin, and offered me her hand. Her grip was stronger than most guys' I know. Rhonda was short, stocky, and top-heavy, but seemed entirely at ease with herself, and I immediately decided that she and I would be friends.

"This airport is always fucking crazy," she said, grabbing my bag off the carousel before I could. "Let's get the hell out of here."

Evidently, there was no "putting on airs" with Rhonda.

We walked out of the pavilion directly into a parking lot full of the sorriest excuses for motor vehicles I'd ever seen assembled in one place, with the possible exception of a junkyard.

Nearly all the cars were old, small, dented, and rusty, and made my station wagon seem like a Mercedes by comparison. (I was later told that it was inadvisable to own a nice vehicle in a climate that was basically designed to destroy any metal object as quickly as possible.)

Of all these crappy vehicles, Rhonda's was the crappiest: a mid-'80s model Toyota pickup that was so degraded by rust, I was amazed it could hold itself together. My impression was that it had at some point been blue, but it was impossible to tell for sure. I carefully placed my guitar and suitcase in the one spot of the truck bed that seemed to have enough metal remaining to hold them up.

We sat down in the cab, and before I could scarcely settle myself, Rhonda handed me a sweaty, cold can of beer.

"Here — you need this," she said as a statement of fact. Seated in the driver's seat, she popped one open for herself and took a long pull. I stared at her, speechless.

"Buckle your seatbelt, though," she said. "They don't care if you drink and drive, but they'll pull you for not wearing a seatbelt."

Off we went into the warm night. With the 4-cylinder engine of the Toyota whining in protest and the thick air whipping through the cab, we lurched through the tropical countryside of St. Croix — on the left side of the road, much to my surprise. The little truck rattled and vibrated at what I considered to be breakneck speed, but Rhonda and I chatted casually, gulping down the cold Budweiser like water.

Turns out that Rhonda was my age and a Northeasterner. She had decided, much to the chagrin of her parents, to forfeit her blue-blooded inheritance in Massachusetts in favor of the wilds of the Caribbean. Arriving in St. Croix only about two years earlier, Rhonda had made a life for herself, first working for a financial advisor, then crewing on Soggy Beard boats, then running the bar. Over the next few weeks, I would find her to be a first-rate, hard-nosed businesswoman, a tough bar-back, a loyal, protective friend, and, like most everybody in our age group, a master partier. Every merchant and street person in downtown Christiansted knew and respected Rhonda, and although she was half my size, I considered her to be my personal bodyguard.

It was dark now, and as I watched the headlights illuminate the turpentine, manchineel, and "monkey-no-climb" trees of the rainforest through which we were passing, I wondered if I was really there, in that rattle-trap truck, on this strange island. Only six hours ago, I'd boarded a plane at Nashville International Airport, and although it was less than ideal, the world all made sense. I was quite accustomed to living in a tiny apartment and scraping to get by. Now, the haze of airline travel, the smell of the thick air, and the shock of my alien surroundings had me nearly sick with sensory overload. My world had been turned on its head. The only thing that seemed comforting to me was my guitar, and the card catalog of 400 songs filed neatly in my brain. In that, I had confidence.

As I watched asphalt rush by through the rusted-out holes in the floorboard, Rhonda told me that I should expect a warm and curious reception at the bar. She explained that The Mizzenmast was the premier live-music joint in Christiansted and the most popular nightspot among expatriate locals and tourists from the mainland. Each music act was booked for a month or two, so if somebody sucked, the island was stuck with him or her for a while. A bad musician resulted in lowered morale and anemic drink sales. People became grumpy, which was forbidden in the Caribbean.

So according to Rhonda, the guy before me sucked. The locals were equal parts excited to see what they were getting next and relieved the other guy was gone.

"Oh my God, you'd better be good," Rhonda said as she downed another beer, her blond hair blowing across her face. "I already like you better than the bozo who left today, but you'd better be good. I seriously can't handle another month of shitty music and lousy tips."

I sat there in stunned silence, trying not to let my feet slip through the floorboard like Fred Flintstone as I wondered what in the world I'd gotten myself into. Every new gig was stressful and required intestinal fortitude, but they were also usually just a night or two. I could always take the money and escape the next day. But here, there was no escape for two solid months, either for the musician or the audience of locals.

"I'll do the best I can," I yelled to Rhonda over the road noise. "I guess it's up to you guys to decide if it's any good or not."

"Please, God, tell me you do some Buffett."

"Yeah, some."

"Then you'll be fine," she grinned, clearly relieved. "Pull out some obscure Buffett every now and then, let people buy you drinks, and you'll be in like Flynn. This last idiot didn't know any Buffett at all. Not even fucking 'Margaritaville.'"

Leaving the rainforest, we passed a hand-painted sign that read, "Beer-drinking pigs turn here," and pointed up a side road. I couldn't tell whether the words were meant to help the beer-drinking pigs know where to turn, or for humans who wanted to witness pigs drink beer, but decided to save that question for another day. The landscape seemed to become arid almost immediately, and as we topped a hill, the lights of Christiansted spread out before me.

6

PALMETTO

The Mizzenmast was on the second floor of a three-story building on Queen Cross Street, wedged between similar structures in the heart of Christiansted. In the dim streetlights, I could see that the building was painted a pale yellow with simple white accents. Three matching yellow awnings extended past the roofline and covered the patio of the bar that overlooked the street below. A stucco and wrought iron staircase descended from the southern end of the patio and terminated on the walkway of the adjacent building, which I found interesting. I can only imagine the arguments that went on between these two building owners when The Mizzenmast building was constructed years ago.

"Hey, mon! Get your staircase off my walkway!"

"That's not your walkway! That's everybody's walkway!"

On the first floor was a clothing shop. Glancing around, I noticed that first floors seemed to be reserved for retail while second floors tended toward business offices and restaurants. The third floor of The Mizzenmast looked like a wooden box that had been hastily plopped onto the roof of the second story. It was only about half the width of the building, painted white instead of yellow, and was about as unattractive as any structure within view.

"That's your apartment," Rhonda said, pointing at the third-floor box.

Of course it is, I thought but didn't say.

Carrying my stuff — essentially one small suitcase, a backpack, and a guitar case — I followed Rhonda through a wrought-iron fence that connected The Mizzenmast with its neighbor on the north side and into the courtyard of what appeared to be a defunct hotel. She led me up two flights of stairs and along an open walkway that ended in a locked door on the other side of the apartment.

"You'll have to go through our office to get to your room," Rhonda explained as she unlocked the door. "I know it's weird, but that's the best we can do."

Indeed, she flipped on the light to reveal a small, tidy office with two workspaces. On the other side of the room, Rhonda unlocked another door that led into my home for the next eight weeks.

It looked like a frat boy's room, complete with a stained, 1970s-era shag carpet, a dorm fridge, a double bed, a threadbare, sagging couch, and a blaring window air conditioner that sounded like a Model-T Ford. Dusty, yellowed faux-wood blinds covered the windows, and the exposed metal roof sloped up and toward the front of the building. Ghostly cobwebs in each corner of the ceiling swayed in the breeze provided by a fan hanging from the center joist. Along the wall facing the couch, an ancient Magnavox television set featured a pair of equally decrepit rabbit ears on top. Drawn into the thick dust covering the TV's screen was a cartoon penis, complete with balls. The words "Clean me" were scrawled beside it.

"Ahhh," I said with a broad smile. "Home crap home!"

Under the carpet came the rhythmical thump of a bass drum over a PA system and unintelligible singing.

"You're directly over the bar, so you probably won't want to be here during business hours when you're not playing," Rhonda said as she made a quick inspection of the space. "I need to get downstairs and help Kenny get ready for tonight. We open in an hour, so come down whenever you want." She handed me a set of door keys and walked toward the door.

"What time is maid service?" I called after her.

"Whenever you get your ass up and do it," she responded without turning around. The door closed, and I was alone.

While the outside surroundings were alien to me, the inside was not. I'd been housed in less-than-luxurious accommodations plenty of times and was unfazed. I peeked out a grungy window that faced north and strained to see something that resembled an ocean. In the near distance, I thought I saw some bobbing lights in blackness, but I wasn't sure.

As was my custom, I wanted to get myself squared away before relaxing, so I decided to start with putting away my clothes, what little I had. When I opened the top drawer of a scuffed-up dresser, a scurrying sound and flash of brown sent a hot flash of terror up my neck.

It appeared to be an absurdly huge cockroach.

The thing darted in a few crazy directions before defying all commonly accepted laws of nature related to roaches and took to the air, flying directly at my face. With a screech usually reserved for witches and bobcats, I ducked and contorted in slow motion, rotating in space like Keanu Reeves dodging bullets in *The Matrix*. I could feel the disturbance of the air as the insect flew past my face with the sound of a tiny helicopter. It buzzed to a corner of the 10-foot, exposed metal ceiling where it landed and dangled like a wobbly brown icicle, ready to drop onto my head at any moment.

"Holy Mother of God!" I yelled in the bug's general direction. "What in God's name are you?!"

I learned later that night that it was referred to as a palmetto bug, which created a lively and unappealing debate over whether it was an American or German cockroach. Now at the time, I had no idea what a palmetto bug was nor was aware that they were as common in the Caribbean as mosquitos in Tennessee, and that I would have to learn to coexist. I just assumed that this one particular individual was an anomaly, perhaps a mutation created by the radioactivity of a nearby nuclear reactor or the evil co-mingling of a roach and a vampire bat. In either case, it had to die and immediately.

In a panic, I glanced around the room, trying to find something with which to knock it down while also keeping a wary eye on its location. As I looked for a proper projectile, I grabbed a broom and held the business end like Captain America's shield in case the giant roach decided to fly at me again. Nothing I could locate had the heft I needed to dislodge my opponent without also damaging the room.

That wouldn't have mattered much anyway.

Suddenly, it occurred to me. I darted into the tiny bathroom, clicked on the light, and found what I was looking for — toilet paper. Perfect! Now armed with a deadly roll of Charmin and a broom, I crept within striking distance and fired the projectile at the insect. Billowing three feet of tissue behind it like a comet, the Extra-Soft 2-ply Charmin nailed the bug, angled downward, and bounced off a lamp, upending it with a crash. The evil beast flopped to the floor, and I rushed at it with my sneakered feet.

"Die, bastard!" I yelled as my foot came down.

CRUNCH.

I jumped back with another witch screech and did a kind of strange tribal dance of disgusted horror. Had anyone been watching, my Man Card would've been revoked immediately.

Welcome to the Caribbean.

〜

By the time I had finished using a disproportionally large handful of Charmin to clean up the disaster left by the palmetto bug's violent death, it was time to take a shower and head downstairs to the bar. I fumbled with locking the doorknob in the darkness of the office (because I didn't know where the light switch was) and then began navigating a maze of walkways and staircases until finally locating the back entrance of the bar, guided by "She Drives Me Crazy" by Fine Young Cannibals blaring over the sound system. I entered the door and followed a narrow hallway that opened into the main room.

The Mizzenmast was a compact bar with low ceilings, plank-wood walls, and stone and stucco accents. Various pieces of maritime paraphernalia were scattered about, and everything seemed old and weathered. The tables and chairs were wicker worn smooth by the salt air that drifted unimpeded through open windows and doors. I had the distinct impression that nothing new — except for the human inhabitants and a collection of neon beer signs — had been added to the establishment since the days of the pirates themselves.

As soon as Rhonda spotted me, she muted the sound system and banged the flat of her hand on the bar, then whistled with incredible shrill volume through her teeth, drawing the attention of the patrons.

"Hey, listen up, everybody! That's Mark Johnson! He's our new entertainment, and he's fucking awesome! (She didn't know this at all.) This is gonna be the best two months of the year!"

She pointed at me, and all conversation quieted with every set of eyes turned in my direction. I considered fleeing but had no idea where I would go.

"Howdy, y' all," I said to the room with a lame wave. "I guess you're stuck with me for a while."

The room was silent save the hum of the ceiling fans. Somewhere in the street outside, a dog barked.

"We're celebrating tonight!" yelled Rhonda and just like that, the music was back on, and people resumed their conversations.

With beads of sweat gathering on my forehead, I collapsed into an empty stool midway down the bar top. Before I could settle my behind into the contours of the seat, a shot glass appeared before me — blam!

"What can I get you, Mr. Mark?" said Rhonda, who was clearly enjoying herself.

I would've liked to have said, "Martini, shaken not stirred" like James Bond, but I wasn't much of a cocktail drinker. In a panic, I made my first mistake of many that night.

"I dunno. Choose something to get me started."

There were multiple mistakes with this response. Not only did I immediately cede control over my drink choice to Rhonda, but I also implied that I was willing to proceed beyond the first offering. I would live to regret this.

"How about a Jäger?"

"Well, I don't know. What's a Jäger?"

"Oh, crap — you've never had a Jager?!" Rhonda said, incredulous. "It's Jägermeister. It's the best German liqueur ever. That's what we're doing!"

Before I could reply, she grabbed an odd, squarish bottle out of a cooler and poured brown liquid into my shot glass. The stuff was ice cold, and the glass began to sweat.

I did the shot, and she was right — it was good. It had a woody, licorice flavor, and didn't seem all that dangerous.

This isn't so bad. I like this. I like Jägermeister.

I had scarcely swallowed before Rhonda was refilling the glass. *Glug, glug, glug.*

"Hold My Hand" by Hootie and the Blowfish was now playing, which annoyed me slightly because, in the late '80s, they often played the same venues in Eastern North Carolina as MJ &

Frenz. Not that I was jealous of their success. Okay, maybe I was a little jealous.

A man dropped into the chair next to me. "I'm Frank Foley," he said, offering me a thick, hairy hand. "Nice to meet you. I'm the 'Norm' of this bar."

I didn't say it, but he did kind of remind me of Norm, of *Cheers* fame. Mid- to late-30s, thick glasses, on the overweight side of stocky, a thick head of wiry black hair with a spray of gray in the front. He had an upper-Midwest accent and friendly look about him.

"I'm Mark. I'm the musician of this bar. Well, starting tomorrow, anyway."

We made some small talk, and he told me he worked at Hess Oil Co. as a harbormaster, directing boats from a tower that overlooks the water like an air-traffic controller directs airplanes on a tarmac. But I could tell something else was on his mind and it didn't take him long to get around to it.

"So, let's get down to business," Frank said, watching me carefully. "The guy who just left didn't play any Buffett and was an asshole. I come here nearly every night just to keep myself sane, but I can't handle another season of crappy music. So... can you do any Buffett?"

He stared at me through his Harry Caray glasses.

I drained Jäger No. 2 and smiled. "Sure, I do some."

"Like what?" he asked, clearly not satisfied yet. "Give me some details."

"Let's go at it this way. Why don't you name a Buffett song you like, and I'll tell you if I do it."

Frank's eyes narrowed, and he leaned closer.

"Okay. 'Changes in Latitudes.'"

"Yep."

"'A Pirate Looks at 40.'"

"Yep."

"'Son of a Son of a Sailor.'"

"Don't waste my time." I met Frank's glare without blinking. He leaned back and grinned.

"Okay, okay," he said. "Let's dig a little deeper."

"Bring it."

"'One Particular Harbor.'"

"Yep."

"'Tin Cup Chalice.'"

"Yessir."

"'Cheeseburger in Paradise.'"

"Please." I yawned and stretched. Hootie was in the background, annoying me.

"How about 'Nautical Wheelers,' and 'Havana Daydreaming'?" Frank asked, his eyes now wide.

"In my sleep," I replied.

He was starting to sweat. "Yeah, but I bet you can't do 'Honey Do,'" he whispered. "Nobody does 'Honey Do.'"

I gently placed my glass on the wooden bar and turned to face Frank square on.

"I'll see your 'Honey Do,' and raise you a 'Dreamsicle,' 'Door Number Three,' 'Death of an Unpopular Poet,' and 'Chanson pour Les Petite Enfants.' Care to continue?"

"Holy shit!" Frank shouted, leaping off the stool. "We got us a winner here! Hot damn! Josh! Lilly! Chris! Get over here and meet this guy!"

The crowd around me grew. *Blam*, went the shot glass. *Glug, glug, glug. Blam! Glug, glug, glug.*

As the night wore on, things got a little weird. I was introduced to a gaggle of regulars whose names instantly vanished between the disconnected synapses of my rapidly diminishing brain function. Rhonda's sunburned, laughing face kept pouring Jäger shots, and any good judgment that may have existed within me two hours earlier — and might have produced the words, "No, thanks. I've had enough" — had been thoroughly subdued and silenced by the alcohol. Dreadlocked Rastas spoke to me in a dialect that would've been difficult to decipher had I been sober. Tanned college coeds chatted about their sororities and their boyfriends and other things I couldn't have cared less about.

Meanwhile, a local musician named Jim Brady had begun playing to fill the two-day gap between me and the asshole who didn't play any Buffett and had whipped the crowd into a frenzy. Brady was a St. Croix legend, and luckily for me, he usually performed on the other side of the island. Nevertheless, he was so good that worry and self-doubt began trying to slip into my brain through a back entrance that wasn't being carefully blocked by over-exuberant German liqueur doormen. My self-doubt, however, was now compounded by a new fear: my drunkenness. Somewhere down deep, a voice was speaking to me.

Johnson, look at what you're doing to yourself, the voice said. *This is your first night! You haven't even opened your guitar case, and these people think you're great. Tomorrow, they might absolutely hate you, and then you'll not only be bad, but you'll be a bad drunk! Stop drinking!*

I refused to listen to my own sound counsel. *Glug, glug, glug. Blam!*

More locals introduced themselves to me, and by now, I was watching myself having embarrassing conversations with people from a vantage point outside my own body, somewhere near the ceiling. Over the ring of Jim Brady's guitar, I could just make out the ridiculous and nonsensical things I was saying and was yelling at myself to shut the hell up and, above all, stop drinking. My tiny sober consciousness couldn't quite get through to my drunk self, which was clearly dominating the situation.

Somewhere inside my brain, I was shaking my head in wonder. Within my first four or five hours in the Caribbean, I had already been attacked and nearly murdered by a giant demon bug, and then transformed into a drunken buffoon by some crazy German liqueur, having played not a single note.

It all finally ended, though I have no recollection of how or when. I somehow managed to get myself back into the upstairs apartment, collapsed onto the bed, and fell into a fitful, tilting, swirling sleep.

~

AT AROUND 6 A.M., I LATER ESTIMATED, MY EYES opened. I was face down, lying diagonally across the bed. Something was in my right hand. I looked and found I was holding a napkin with a few words handwritten in ink. They had been blotted out by liquid, though, and were illegible, forever to remain a mystery.

Cindy Crawford's phone number?

A winning lottery sequence?

I'd never know.

Soft morning light was just beginning to filter through the blinds on the window. At that moment, my body realized that it was awake, and this wasn't a good thing.

In fact, it was a bad thing.

The exuberant, jolly, licorice-flavored Germans wearing wooden clogs and dancing arm in arm from the night before had changed. They were no longer jolly. Now, they were mean and ugly. They had morphed into Nazis, pushing and shoving my brain against the inside of my skull, and my stomach against my ribcage, blowing shrill whistles, leading mean, snarling dogs, and demanding to see my papers. When I tried to close my eyes and go back to sleep, the Nazis yelled obscenities and forced open my eyelids. When I tried to sit up, they fired their weapons into the air and shoved me onto the bed. In spite of their screaming and shoving, I rolled off to the grungy floor and crawled — yes, crawled — the interminable six feet from my bed to the bathroom. Hanging my 40-pound-melon-of-a-head into the toilet, I did as the Nazis ordered before crawling back under the barbed wire and whizzing bullets to the bed but couldn't manage to hoist my body back into it.

This process repeated itself over and over, crawling back and forth. After at least an hour of expelling every last remaining molecule of Jägermeister, I bribed one of the Nazi guards into letting me place a call to Rhonda from an old rotary phone on the bedside table. She picked up the line sounding chipper. "Hello?"

"Rhonda, for God's sake, it's Mark," I croaked. "I think there was something in those shots. I think I might be dying. Seriously, I'm not joking. Can you come bring me a glass of cold water?"

Rhonda laughed cheerfully.

"Oh, silly," she said. "You'll be fine. Can't wait to see you play tonight! See you at around 8:30? Bye!" Click.

It was more than I could take. The Nazis began yelling at me again, and I passed out on the floor, leaving the phone receiver dangling.

7

STEPS

When I came to an hour later, the Nazis were gone, replaced by a dull, thumping heartbeat in both my head and stomach. Although I was nowhere near normal, I could now tell that I wasn't going to die.

I staggered to the window and squinted into the morning sunlight. At the end of the street, shimmering blue water was visible between two rooftops. The Caribbean Sea! Instinctively, I knew that's where I needed to be. Nothing else would do.

I pulled on my swim trunks, a T-shirt, and Wayfarer sunglasses, navigated through the still vacant office, and walked in a delicate straight line down the steps into the courtyard of the old hotel. Gecko lizards scattered in every direction within the fallen leaves of the big mango tree as I stumbled toward the street.

"Can y'all please go into my room and eat all those giant bugs?" I asked them but received no response.

After fumbling with the lock on the wrought iron gate, I walked into the streets of Christiansted, a long-haired country boy, a mountaineer from the highlands of the North Carolina Appalachians who now had to pretend to be a Caribbean club entertainer. It seemed I had lived a lifetime since my plane had touched down less than 24 hours before. I was hungover, confused, and petrified, and I had about half a day to pull myself together.

Again, I felt the inexplicable pull of something at the end of the street. I flip-flopped my way toward a glistening patch of blue.

~

LONELINESS MANIFESTS ITSELF IN MYRIAD WAYS.

There is the loneliness of being in an empty house while your spouse is away. Or of hiking alone in the woods, out of earshot of the nearest highway. Or of not being in a romantic relationship during the holidays.

These all apply and are all perfectly good examples of the word.

But there's nothing quite so lonely as finding yourself on an island — in another country, for all practical purposes — some 1,800 miles away from the nearest people you know and love. Of the 50,000 people who live on said island, probably only one can recognize you or call you by name. It is entirely possible, in fact, that not one other person of those 50,000 is, at that moment in time, as utterly anonymous, unfamiliar, and isolated as are you.

Now throw in a head-banging hangover, and you've really got something.

As I flip-flopped down Queen Cross Street, store proprietors and employees were greeting one another and entering their shops. Every face was that of a stranger, and the lilting Cruzan dialect of the indigenous population was unintelligible, if only slightly.

Yes, there was enormous excitement. Just the word "Caribbean" alone carries with it the promise of adventure. Pirates! Tanned damsels! Shimmering teal waters!

I felt confident that I might experience these lofty expectations if I could simply get through the next two or three hours of nausea and the nagging feeling that everyone in this town was noticing my state of total confusion and disorientation. It felt like I was wearing one of those old-time sandwich banners over my torso; the front said, "First day in the islands," and the back said "Clueless." I had absolutely no idea of where I was going or what I was doing, and at the moment, my main ambition was to stay upright and replace the green hue of my skin with something less reptilian.

I had heard mention of some type of resort that was on a small island in Christiansted Harbor. This was a cay, they said, but you pronounce it "key." There was a hotel out there — Hotel on the Cay — with food and a nice beach, they had said. (I was fairly distrustful of whatever "they" had said, because they had said it the night before, and nothing from the night before could be trusted.)

So, with the mindlessness of running water, I simply followed the downward slope of the street until it ended. There, in broad, sunny daylight, was the Caribbean Sea in all its ridiculous glory. Dozens of anchored sailboats rocked gently as a slight wind created ripples across an otherwise docile surface. The air was perfumed by a combination of salt, diesel fuel, fish, and suntan lotion. My polarized sunglasses created a living vision of high-definition color contrasted against enormous cotton-ball-white clouds hanging within reach, it seemed.

I'll have to admit that the vista matched my rather absurd imagination, if not exceeding it. I stood gawking until I lost my balance and nearly toppled over, grabbing the side of a building to steady myself.

Not too far out into the harbor was the island, the "cay," I had heard about. It was called Protestant Cay. I noticed a water taxi that seemed to be making regular trips there, so I paid my $3 and climbed aboard the small craft. As we puttered across the harbor, I detected some of my stress beginning to ebb. A pleasant, 78-degree breeze blew through the open cabin of the boat, and I listened as an older tourist couple questioned the captain about his job. Looking back toward the town, I saw pastel residences dotting the hillsides overlooking the harbor, creating even more color on an already absurd canvas that was beyond description.

Upon reaching Protestant Cay, we climbed out onto a small pier. The taxi captain called out "Irie!" u-turned the boat and headed back across the harbor.

I smiled and waved back at him, having no idea what "irie" meant. Before the week was out, I would learn that "irie" in the Caribbean is similar to "aloha" in Hawaii. Whereas both words can work for "hello" and "goodbye," the Caribbean version is also loosely translated to "I'm feeling good," "I'm feeling really good," and "Jeez, I'm stoned, let's get food."

Carrying my flip-flops in my hand, I lurched barefoot across the sand toward what appeared to be a restaurant that faced the beach. I found myself an open table and was approached by the waiter, a middle-aged white guy in a polo shirt and khaki shorts.

"Good morning, sir, and welcome to Hotel on the Cay," the man said in what I surmised was a New York accent. "My name is Norman."

He looked at me closely. "Can I start you with a bloody Mary this morning?"

"Is it that obvious?" I replied with a weak chuckle. "That's embarrassing."

"No judgment here," said Norman. "I've been there. You should try running this place for a day."

Turns out that Norman was the owner of Hotel on the Cay and was a pleasant man. He promised to come see me play at The Mizzenmast as soon as possible.

After the bloody Mary and a small plate of fresh fruit, I made my way across the sand to the water's edge. No crashing surf here — just a docile, crystalline sea lapping at the beach almost apologetically. I didn't take the time to spread out my towel or situate myself. Backpack dropped, shirt and flip-flops in a pile, and I eased in.

Since my childhood on the farm, I had envisioned the waters of the Caribbean to be like that of a warm bath, so I was a bit surprised that it was slightly cool. But with an intense sun radiating down, the water became the perfect temperature within minutes.

Thus began my healing. Time became a nebulous concept as I floated on my back in the buoyant sea, letting the salinity draw the Jägermeister residue out through my skin to disperse harmlessly. I bobbed in the gentle waves and planned my night's gig, growing more confident as time passed. A better hangover cure was never conceived. I was suspended in a lagoon of God's own medicine, and when I emerged, I was myself again.

I HAD SPENT NEARLY TWO HOURS ALTERNATING between floating, drying myself in the sun, and re-applying sunscreen. There was still plenty of time before the start of my gig, so I puttered back across Christiansted Harbor and began exploring some of the shops and trying to decipher the layout of the town. The streets were arranged in a traditional grid, but each block was subdivided with small, unnamed, pedestrian alleys that ran between buildings. Instead of sidewalks, there were covered walkways created by the architecture of the structures.

Like a bear cub on its first outing from the den, I explored only within a small radius centered around The Mizzenmast, careful not to stray very far. After locating a tiny market called

The Alley Galley, where I could purchase a few essentials, I felt better. I had learned how to get to the water, get food, and get supplies. I could survive now. The next order of business was the get some actual sober rest. I hoofed it back to The Mizzenmast.

As I approached the door to the outer office, I could hear voices inside. I tapped the door apologetically and stuck my head in.

"Hi, I'm Mark," I said to the two women seated at desks, a blond and brunette, both probably in their 40s, I estimated. "I'm the new musician. So sorry to bother you, but I'm heading to my room."

"No bother," said the blonde woman with a smile. "I'm Julie. That's Sandra. Just warn us when you've got girls in there so we can pretend not to notice."

"Wow, straight to the point!" I responded as they both laughed. "I will do my best. Nice to meet you both."

I fumbled with the key but managed to get into the relative safety of my room. Even with the door closed, I could still hear the two women giggling.

I collapsed on the bed. The Caribbean sun, saltwater, humid air, lingering hangover, and sheer surges and drops of adrenaline had done me in, and I fell into a wonderful, dream-free sleep. When I awoke three hours later, it was just getting dark outside.

I was groggy but felt 100-percent better. Time to start prepping. I would go on in about 90 minutes.

IT WAS 8:55 PM.

"Testing, one, two, one two," I said into my Shure SM58 microphone. "Check, check."

The sound was surprisingly decent, provided by the two large speakers suspended from the ceiling by nautical rope. A floor monitor hummed at my feet. Behind me was a wood-plank wall with a red hand-painted sign with gold lettering that read "The Mizzenmast." Within reach of my right hand was a compact amplifier into which my microphone, guitar, and a house CD player were plugged.

The plain-Jane, cutaway Takamine guitar felt good in my hands, reassuring me that we made a great team. No matter where on the planet you plopped me down, if I could sit on a stool with my guitar on my knee, I felt right.

A large crowd was already in the room, undoubtedly a result of Rhonda talking me up and building the drama of opening night. She and Frank Foley stood near the front door, speaking to each other but looking at me.

I made slight adjustments to the tone and volume of my guitar, plucking a soft chord or two, both to fine-tune the sound and to build the anticipation of the audience. On the floor, between my feet and the monitor, were the two cardboard setlists — scrawled in Sharpie permanent ink — that traveled with me. I never followed any particular order, but as I played a song, would glance down and choose the next from the dog-eared lists.

The big hand on the neon Bud Light sign above the bar clicked over to 9 pm.

Here we go.

The choice of the first song of an opening night gig is a tricky matter. It should be impressive but not a biggie, not a closer. It should be a harbinger of good music ahead without giving away the store. You never waste a crowd-pleaser on an early-evening crowd (unless you're already famous), yet with this number, I knew I needed to bring something.

I chose James Taylor's "T-Bone." Complicated, funky, odd, comfortable in my vocal range, and a vehicle for some interesting guitar work. It wasn't a well-known song but was nonetheless infectious. I took a deep breath and clipped my old-gold

Kyser capo onto the second fret of the guitar. Without any introductions, I began.

About 15 seconds in, Rhonda leaped into the air and started banging Frank's shoulder with awkward punches. With enormous smiles, the two exchanged a mighty high-five.

The mix of the amplifier was fantastic, clear and warm, and the new D'Addario strings were bright. I was in good voice, with no sign of a nervous quiver.

Halfway through the song, "T-Bone" breaks down into a Beethoven-esque instrumental pattern where, if you don't know the tune, you believe it might just end. Just then, it roars back to life with a circular chord progression that's an irresistible call to action for motionless feet. It worked as planned.

By now, bodies were streaming in off the street and into the main entrance. I could hear Rhonda's excited chatter over my own singing, a phenomenon that would persist throughout my stay in St. Croix.

I ended the song to wild applause and a huge, internal sigh of relief. I was no longer an unknown commodity.

Her wild mane of sun-bleached hair swinging to and fro, Rhonda practically flattened a few patrons in a mad sprint to the stage. She grabbed the mike as I smiled and acted like I knew what she was doing, which I didn't.

"Ladies and gentlemen, this is Mark Johnson, from Nashville fucking Tennessee," she shouted, creating low-frequency feedback that rattled windows two blocks away. "All I can say is, we're going to have a load of fucking fun over the next eight weeks!"

Well, alrighty then. I would learn during my residency that when Rhonda was excited, f-bombs would be released like doves at the opening ceremony of the Olympics, flying haphazardly in all directions. The Caribbean was not for the faint of heart or the delicate of sensibilities.

A chorus of loud cheers arose, and I could see that I may as well skip to the crowd favorites. The usual slow arc of the night's show had been sped up considerably by Rhonda's enthusiastic announcement.

"Glad to be here, y'all!" I drawled through the P.A. system and launched the distinctive, opening changes of Buffett's "Son of a Son of a Sailor." A hurrah went up immediately, as if by magic, and I silently thanked J.B. for making my life easier.

I caught Frank Foley's eye and gave him a sly wink. In return, he held his bottle of beer up in a salute and shouted, "Thank you!" Beer bottles were being clinked together as people made unintelligible toasts to happy things. Voices quickly locked onto the chorus of the song until the phrase "son of a son of a SAIL-or" was surely echoing down the length of Queen Cross Street and exhausting itself across the glassy waters of the harbor.

In that moment, the loneliness and uncertainty of the past 24 hours shrank into a molecule and disappeared with a tiny pop. For the next two months — and for better or worse — I was home.

8

PIRATES

Ah, the exotic, mysterious Caribbean Islands.
Americans tend to think of the Caribbean as little more than a worry-free vacation destination, a gigantic tanning booth with steel drum music ever-present in the background. But we generally don't know any details. It's that area "down there," all those dots on a map between North and South America. Puerto Rico and Jamaica might be down there. Possibly Bermuda, but we're not sure.

The U.S. Virgin Islands — St. Thomas, St. John, and St. Croix — are even more homogenized in our collective imaginations. They don't seem as cool or "serious" as some of the other Caribbean islands, but more like a version of Disney World scattered across a trio of landmasses that Uncle Sam was able to purchase as part of some larger, more important deal. The U.S.V.I. come off as the winter home of fat cat Wall Street millionaires and a four-hour refueling stop for cruise ships destined for somewhere better and even more exotic.

But the overlying image of the Virgin Islands is one of vaguely disinterested confusion. In other words, we don't think about them very often, but when we do, we're a little annoyed by our own ignorance in the matter.

Americans in general: And how, exactly, are the Virgin Islands part of the U.S.? What the heck is a "territory?" Does this mean Cruzans (the collective term for St. Croix natives) have to adhere to American laws and pay American taxes? Is that spelled "Cruzan" or "Crucian" and who came up with that word anyway? If Cruzans are American, why are they driving on the left-hand side of the road? What's going on, here? Never mind, I'm not that worried about it.

In 1995, though, none of these things bothered me, either, or mattered at all. I just wanted a sandwich, to forget about my troubles in Nashville, to not mess up on stage, and to attract as much female companionship as possible.

It was Day 3 on the island, and after waking up somewhat sober and well-rested, I determined that this would be a day of exploration. I strapped on my backpack, slipped into my flip-flops, and headed onto the street, geckos scattering before me as usual. The sun and sky overhead were brilliant, and 75 degrees in January had never felt better. I had $27 in my pocket courtesy of last night's tip jar, creating a sense of empowerment and pride reserved only for artists and musicians. To feed yourself entirely on the merits of your own talent and all those hours of practice and frustration is, well, pretty OK. I bee-lined to a tiny outdoor cafe and ordered myself the largest, most audacious breakfast on the menu to celebrate.

I decided to go fancy — eggs benedict — and chatted with the proprietor, an old, leathery Englishman named Harold, as I ate.

"Heard you last night," the old man said as he wiped an adjacent table. "Just in the street here as I was finishing a spot of work on the shop. You sounded quite nice. You should be quite chuffed with yourself."

"Ah, many thanks, Harold."

"Any Beatles in the repertoire?" he asked. "Or Dave Clark 5, perhaps?"

"Beatles, yes, Dave Clark, no. Give me a heads-up next time you're within earshot, and I'll do a Beatles for you."

"Brilliant," he said. "Have a lovely day."

"Indeed I shall, Harold," I responded, smiling thoughtfully. "Indeed, I shall."

I'm pretty sure the only times I ever used the words "indeed" and "shall" in the same sentence was while conversing with Harold. I've never used "chuffed," though. (Although, I guess I just did.)

≈

AFTER SAYING MY GOODBYES TO HAROLD, I purchased a disposable Kodak camera from the shop next door and embarked onto my mission of discovery. Within minutes, it dawned on me that St. Croix was more than rum punch and Coppertone.

There was a grittiness that was easy for TV and travel brochures to omit and a depth that was impossible to include. Christiansted was a claustrophobic jumble of buildings, narrow streets, and hidden alleys. From my home base — The Mizzen-mast — down to the waters of Christiansted Harbor, the road was narrow but fairly tidy and appealing to tourists, a cluster of jewelry, liquor, and souvenir shops.

But as I looked closer, many of the buildings seemed old. Like, really old.

Sure, there were plenty of modern shops and businesses, but almost without fail, they were housed in structures of a common architecture — Dutch, I learned later — that appeared to be cracked and crumbling with an indeterminate history of baking under the equatorial sun. Upon closer inspection, I could see that even where the stucco had fallen away on several buildings, multiple layers of paint belied a long heritage. It was like examining the strata of an exposed cross-section of soil like they do on TV documentaries to date a meteorite strike or some Biblical event.

It occurred to me that this wasn't Disney World, designed exclusively for the amusement of late 20th Century tourists and sun worshippers. To the contrary, as I walked through the streets of Christiansted, my feet were covering the same ground that once ran with the violently shed blood of Carib and Tairo Indians, Spanish explorers, French and Danish colonists, and a bloodthirsty ilk of privateers, buccaneers, and English pirates. That very route was also undoubtedly trodden by thousands of black slaves toiling in the sugar, tobacco, and rum trades.

As you may have guessed, I didn't know any this at the time. I would discover it later. But it was clear that once I ventured outside the "safe" area of Queens Cross Street into the non-tourist parts of town, I was viewed with suspicion by the Cruzan locals. It was as if I was being sized up to determine whether I represented yet another invading force.

It was a valid question, and you can't blame them.

The history of the U.S.V.I is one of constant turmoil and uncertainty, starting in the late 1400s when Christopher Columbus landed at the mouth of the Salt River in St. Croix and was repelled by a barrage of arrows fired by unwelcoming Carib Indians.

Columbus: OK, boys, drop those paddles in and let's head up this river. Ready? Go! One, two, three, four...

Carib Indians: Nope. (Release a barrage of arrows.)

Columbus: Shit! Back up, back up, back up!

From then until its purchase from Denmark by the U.S. in 1917, the islands were being bickered over. Being the largest and more or less isolated from its closest neighbors, St. Croix was arguably the most abused of all, repeatedly invaded, conquered, resettled, invaded again, and conquered again. The island was like a shiny red tricycle being fought over by a group of preschoolers on the playground, in this case, the Tairos and Caribs (from which the Caribbean gets its name), Spanish, French, Danish, and English. It's not like anyone actually wanted to live there so much as they desired to possess it for political leverage or as a staging area to launch military assaults.

As if the near lawlessness and cruelty of the occupying nation weren't bad enough, piracy was rampant from around the mid-1600s through most of the 18th Century. Back then, a bunch of loot was worthless unless you could get it to a trading port or back to your country of origin, and the only way was oversea. Unless you were fortunate or had the fastest ship around, your loot soon became somebody else's loot, and you became dead.

So if you lived in the Caribbean during those years, you would've found both land and sea unsafe. Somebody was continually trying to kill you, rob you, or enslave you.

I can imagine this was a real bummer for each subsequent population that believed they had found the perfect place to put down roots.

Carib Indian, reclining in lounge chair on St. Croix beach, drink in hand: Wow, I'm glad we ran that Columbus bozo off a few months ago because this place is fantastic. Look at that teal water and feel this temperate breeze.

French explorer, holding sword to Indian's neck: Give me all your loot and get out.

Carib Indian: Dang.

One year later...

French explorer, reclining in lounge chair on St. Croix beach, drink in hand: Wow, this place is fantastic. Look at that teal water and feel this temperate breeze. I'm glad those Indian bozos are gone.

English pirate, holding sword to Spanish explorer's neck: Give me all your loot and get out.

French explorer: Dang.

Actually, the idea of seriously vacationing in the Caribbean didn't come around until the mid-20th Century. I guess the travel agents figured the pirates had finally died off and it was safe, so they began promoting the islands in the way they're still presented today. Predictably, this resulted in an influx of whites moving to the U.S.V.I. to run tourist businesses, which probably felt like another hostile takeover to the indigenous population who were only a few generations removed from the real thing.

This could've accounted for what was viewed as the rampant corruption of the local government and, more specifically, police. I was told — from more than one resident — never to call the police for anything lest you found yourself ignored, ridiculed, or possibly even locked up. Rumor had it that the cops were puppets of local drug dealers and otherwise shady business-people and were entirely unsympathetic to the whites that constituted a tiny percentage of the island's demographic. (I like to believe that the St. Croix police in 2019 are brave, lovely, fair-minded people.)

Rhonda recounted a story of a night, prior to my arrival, when she was forced to call the police to have an unruly patron ejected from The Mizzenmast. After the police arrived and interviewed the troublemaker — a local Rasta — they proceeded to kick Rhonda out of her own bar, leaving the guy there to enjoy his drink.

"My guess is that he was a drug dealer and these officers were getting kickbacks from his business," Rhonda said. "I was lucky they didn't arrest me."

Another eye-opener for me was the Rasta community. On TV, they are usually portrayed as fun-loving, music-playing ambassadors of goodwill, always happy to welcome the white tourist with open arms to their postcard-like home.

Although I did know a couple guys who fit this stereotype, many of the Rastas I encountered scared the hell out of me. My interaction with them usually involved being approached on the street for money or solicited for ganja or some other type of drug, either to buy or sell. Honestly, I don't think these guys were practicing the Rastafarian religion as it was intended, but rather were taking advantage of the weed component. Real Rastafarians, you see, famously use cannabis as part of their religious practice, meant to create some type of inner self-awareness. But among the less devout, this becomes a free pass to party and stay stoned out of your mind.

There were a few times that I mistakenly veered out of the "safe" zone and into areas frequented by Rasta gangs. Had I looked like an ordinary tourist, I would've probably been mugged or worse. Instead, these guys lounged in groups like a pride of lazy lions, staring at me impassively through glassy red eyes and sucking on their joints. Resisting the urge to run, I simply stared back defiantly and strolled on past.

BY THE 1990S, TOURISM WAS THE LARGEST INDUSTRY on St. Croix, followed by oil refining and rum production. In fact, a fair percentage of my regular audience comprised white, blue-collar American workers like Frank Foley, who had been shipped down to the islands to operate these facilities. These oil workers melded with tourists, service industry professionals, 20-something adventure seekers, and middle-aged expatriates to create an interesting mix of patrons.

If any particular group exemplified the true spirit of the Caribbean, it was the expatriates. These were usually single men who crewed tourist catamarans, bartended, worked in restaurant kitchens, or simply lived on their own boat anchored in Christiansted harbor. Rarely were they known by their full name, and any story you got from them must be taken with a grain of salt. Some would tell the truth about themselves; most would not. They were the living embodiment of Steve Goodman's classic composition, "Banana Republic." I covered this song at the time and found it strange that I was probably playing it to the very people depicted in the lyrics. (I would include those for you here were it not for the genuine possibility that Goodman's ghost, along with his very much alive lawyer, would probably pounce and make me fork over a huge licensing fee. Go look them up on Google. It's OK. I'll wait.)

See what I mean? Good. Moving along.

There was a sense that the island was a place to live out some inner fantasy and pass the time until it was necessary to re-enter normal society and face the music. They weren't plundering merchant vessels and murdering innocent sailors, but there was no doubt that these were St. Croix's modern-day pirates, hiding out in the tropics where they could literally get by with a pair of shorts, flip-flops, a fishing pole, and an absence of responsibility or true identity.

For example, there was Woody, a wiry, sunbaked 60-year-old who lived on a small sailboat and would often bring his two Chihuahuas, Tiki and Termite, with him to Christiansted in an attempt to ensnare cute female tourists. Woody always had a dirty joke at the ready and would attend most of my shows, shouting out requests for Grateful Dead tunes and sending up tequila shots.

One night over beers, Rhonda told me it was rumored that Woody was a former CEO of an international investment firm who, after a monumental loss of equity and whispers of embezzlement, had faked his own death and fled to the islands under an assumed name. Almost anywhere else, this would sound farfetched, but in St. Croix, it was entirely possible. To us, though, he was just Woody.

Then there was Lonnie, one of the crew members on Soggy Beard's largest catamaran, the Cutlass. Lonnie was in his mid-30s, outgoing and athletic, and famous for wearing a Speedo — yes, *that* kind of Speedo — every day on the boat. To the

European tourists, this was no big deal, but I had a hard time looking in his direction.

"Lonnie. Dude," I'd say, shielding his midsection from view with my hand. "Put on a long t-shirt or something. You're leaving nothing to the imagination."

He would respond by striking a pose with his hands on his hips, like Yul Brenner in "The King and I."

Lonnie was an accomplished swimmer and diver and would often free dive up to 100 feet on one mighty gulp of air. Although I considered him odd-looking with his bleached white hair and matching white porn-star mustache, the guy had an impressive knack of seducing a different woman nearly every day, it seemed. That fact had earned him the nickname "Lon Juan" and the admiration of his buddies.

But there was more to Lonnie than met the eye, Speedo notwithstanding.

One day a few months after I had left St. Croix, Lonnie noticed a strange wire leading into the Cutlass's engine housing while preparing for the day's sail to Buck Island. Turns out, his sharp eye foiled an apparent plot to blow up the boat, as the wire was rigged to spark into the fuel tank upon ignition.

This was extreme, but not unthinkable on St. Croix. Because of Ernest Alvarez's notoriety, it came as little surprise that he had developed his share of enemies on the island over the years.

In any case, Lonnie quickly became elevated to a hero status.

For about a week, that is.

When his name and photo made the paper, it attracted the attention of the U.S. Drug Enforcement Agency. It seems that our mustachioed friend had a cocaine-dealing rap sheet of epic proportions. When the DEA arrived and began investigating, they determined that Lonnie had actually rigged the boat himself, planning all the while to "discover" the threat and save the lives of a dozen tourists, thus making himself a hero. But he didn't count on the press.

Legend has it that Lonnie was last seen boarding an American Airlines flight handcuffed to one of the DEA agents. They say he was smooth-talking one of the cute flight attendants.

The prevalence of drug smugglers and distributors in the Virgin Islands necessitated a certain amount of caution with whom you hung out, and an airtight alibi was necessary in case the po-po came calling. I found it easier and more prudent to keep my casual friendships and acquaintances at arm's length and usually avoided invitations to go do things that sounded strange.

For example, I was once invited to crew a sailboat on a midnight sail to the Salt River Bay. I politely turned the fellow down, as if I knew anything about crewing a sailboat. The next morning, the "coconut telegraph" was abuzz with rumors of a drug bust at the mouth of the Bay. Never saw the sailor again.

To me, Lonnie, Woody, and all these shady guys were the modern-day versions of Sir Frances Drake, Captain Kidd, Black Sam Bellamy, and other notorious pirates and n'er-do-wells who once cruised the waters of the Virgin Islands. They operated on the fringe of the law and, although they eventually paid the piper, they lived life on their own terms.

9

MY MILLENNIUM FALCON MODEL

Let he who is without sin cast the first stone.
(John 8:7)

I'm just saying, don't start getting all judgmental with me. In my shoes, you would've done the same thing.

Don't believe it? Use your imagination for a moment.

You are 16 years old and a figurative 99-pound weakling. You are tall, gangly, skinny, and awkward. You could be compared to that weird, spidery alien that walked off the mother ship in *Close Encounters of the Third Kind* and freaked us all out. You wear heavy sweatshirts and hoodies to make yourself seem more filled out, even in hot weather. You are aware of your awkwardness as you walk down the hallway of the high school, so you continuously practice your stride, trying to make it smooth, unsure of where to hold your hands.

Good-looking girls are a constant source of frustration, mainly because none of them are interested in you as a boyfriend or even as a date. They only go for the shorter, muscular football players with names like "Blake" or "Drew." These guys can grow beards and drive shiny Camaros or pickup trucks with large knobby tires. They always seem tough, fearless, and entirely willing to describe their sexual conquests to a locker-room full of teammates at the drop of a hat.

That's not you.

You've been raised in a Christian home by a loving, hardworking mother and father, and shown by example how a loving married relationship should be. You've been taught to treat girls with respect at all times, never to be aggressive or forward.

Which means you're not getting the girls.

Oh, you are loved as everyone's buddy. You're relatively smart in class and above all, funny — the class clown. Always out front at pep rallies, always being commended publicly for your short stories in Advanced Composition. You are universally admired — and terminally friend-zoned.

That's code for never getting laid.

Wait, I take that back. You've got a pretty good chance of being laid by that one girl, Freda, who plays tuba in the marching band.

Every night, you're haunted by television images of Heather Thomas, Loni Anderson, and Charlene Tilton, and lie in bed awake, wondering how anybody can ever get a hot babe like that. The Farrah Fawcett swimsuit poster tacked to the wall creates a situation where you're repeatedly making up reasons for why your bedroom door is often locked.

Your mom, banging on the door: Why is this locked? Open the door!

You, scrambling: Sorry! I just didn't want Tiger (your cat) to come in and knock over my Millennium Falcon model!

Got the picture yet?

OK, I admit it. I'm describing myself. What made matters worse was that I've always loved females and not just kind of.

I was never one of those little boys who hated little girls. I never joined a "No Girls Allowed" club. To the contrary, from the time I was in preschool, I had a particular affinity for the opposite sex and made every effort to keep their company.

When I reached puberty, I suppose that God thought it might be entertaining (to Him, not me) to give me an unhealthy obsession of the female figure while designing me to resemble a granddaddy longlegs. These two things were in direct conflict with each other.

Until, that is, the Everly Brothers show.

By the time my senior year concluded, that single performance had changed the tide of my established persona. I was now loosely identified as a musician and, better yet, an acoustic guitar player. Why does acoustic matter? Because I could be recruited to play around campfire parties where there was no access to electricity. Instead of the class clown, I became the class entertainer.

This began working to my advantage.

The door to the forbidden and previously locked Room of Hot Women cracked open, if ever so slightly. Somehow, the magic elixir created quite accidentally by my guitar seem to distract cute girls from my string-bean physique, transforming me into a somewhat dateable guy.

By 1995, the forbidden door had been flung wide open. Physically, I had filled out a little, was confident in my own skin, and had affected an air of the slightly dangerous, longhaired traveling troubadour, never staying in one place for very long. At 29, I was no longer a kid.

So, if the previous 10 years had opened the "Hot Women" door, going to St. Croix removed it from its hinges and promptly burned down the entire house.

In most of the United States, the seductive qualities of a guitar are at least slightly tempered by Christian morals and the basic rules of civilized behavior.

Not in the Caribbean in 1995, and certainly not in the Virgin Islands.

I can't imagine any landmass being more improperly named because I'm pretty sure there wasn't a virgin in sight, either male or female. Had Christopher Columbus been aware of its impending future when he bestowed this moniker on the islands in 1493 as a nod to St. Ursula and her 11,000 holy virgins, he might have gone with something else.

I'm referring specifically to the party community here, not the indigenous population as a whole, for whom I can't speak. I'm sure they were upstanding people who were mortified at the goings-on of the current white invaders.

But among the latter, hard drinking and casual sex were viewed as a regional pastime. Not only were good morals not commonly adhered to among the 20-something crowd, they were flat-out shunned. And although I had been raised to know right from wrong, I found myself influenced by the environment and able to turn on and off my proper upbringing whenever it suited me, kind of like a Jekyll and Hyde scenario.

Dr. Jekyll was a friendly young man who every day would stop in and chat with shop keepers and restaurateurs, befriend street beggars, help out as a de facto crew member on the Cutlass, and trade stories with tourists and locals alike. Dr. Jekyll was considerate, displayed the hard-working ethic of a farmer, and was in the market for a good Christian girl with whom to settle down. During the majority of my waking hours, I tended to be Dr. Jekyll and was proud of it.

But emboldened by the false bravado provided by a few beers, rum punches, or drags off a joint, typically late at night after my show was over, Mr. Hyde crept out, determined to make up for all those high school days when he hid beneath his hoodie sweatshirts. Mr. H. took full advantage of the musician mystique, the fairy dust that not only lowered the defenses of certain women but more often than not, put them on the offensive. Hyde was a more-than-willing victim.

This often resulted in what I referred to as the "Office Introduction of Shame" because the only way out of my apartment above The Mizzenmast was through the office. If my overnight guest was still present the next morning, it meant an embarrassing forced introduction to Julie and Sandra. It was morning, after all, and I had reverted back to Dr. Jekyll, complete with Southern manners.

"Good morning, Julie and Sandra, this is Miranda. Miranda, this is Julie and Sandra."

"Good morning, Julie and Sandra, this is Mimsy. Mimsy, this is Julie and Sandra."

"Good morning, Julie and Sandra, this is Joni. Joni, this is Julie and Sandra."

And so on.

Sandra, cheeks reddening, would offer a nervous "Nice to meet you" and quickly return to her work, but not Julie. She relished in every opportunity to mortify me and torture my unfortunate guest by making her stand there in last night's rumpled clothing and have an extended conversation.

"Joni, it's so nice to meet you," she would say, jumping up to shake the girl's hand. She would then launch into a faux-saccharine interrogation of the poor woman as if meeting her son's girlfriend for the first time.

"Are you from around here, honey? How long have you been on the island? Are you in school? What are you studying? You work at the Larimar jewelry store down on the boardwalk? Oh, Sweetie, I love that place! How long have you guys known each other?"

Now it was clear to everyone in the room that Joni and I had known each other a total of about six hours and had barely committed one another's names to memory, but Julie would play dumb and drag out the escape process for as long as she could, shooting me glances and almost imperceptible winks from time to time as my date and I inched closer to the door. As we exited, a chorus of cackling would break out inside. Looking back, I think Julie knew that I was Dr. Jekyll at heart and that this was her way of covertly calling my attention to that fact.

~

No matter how hard I tried, I could never fully commit to the Mr. Hyde side of myself or surrender to the Dark Side.

I wanted to. I really did. For years, I operated within a swirling vortex of immorality, moving about freely and displaying my backstage Professional Musician pass to the Beelzebub security crew whenever required. I had a front-row seat to a never-ending concert of bad behavior, but my gentile Southern upbringing was stubborn. It just wouldn't allow me to go all in.

Oh, I went in. Just not ALL in.

One night, I was faced with the ultimate litmus test for ill repute.

I would fail miserably.

Directly across from The Mizzenmast on Queen Cross Street was a narrow alley that led to one of the many strip clubs on the island at the time, this one called Sails Up. Because of the proximity of the place, the two establishments often shared patrons and even employees.

Two of the Sails Up entertainers, Jasmine and Ryenne, would often attend my show on their off nights. One blond, one brunette, they were both sexy and good-looking, as opposed to some of the other exotic dancers I'd made the mistake of viewing in there, which necessitated an immediate vinegar eye wash.

I became acquainted with Jasmine and Ryenne after finding two homemade coupons for "One Free Lap Dance" in my tip jar one evening. Aside from an occasion a couple of years later in Texas when the founder of the Sonic Drive-In fast food chain bribed me to play another 30 minutes with a crisp $100 bill, the lap dance coupon was the best tip I ever received.

Being an upstanding Southerner of the highest morals, I cashed it in at my first opportunity.

This resulted in a breezy friendship between the two dancers and myself. They attended my shows frequently, often dancing seductively together right in front of me to throw off my concentration, like a prank. It usually worked and I would bungle the lyrics of whatever I was singing.

One night, emboldened by too much of whatever drink someone was buying me, I brazenly invited the girls up to my apartment. To my amazement, they accepted.

I lurched upstairs and quickly made the place presentable when, 10 minutes later, they showed up with a bottle of booze and a fat joint. They were both wearing very short, low-cut, tight-fitting dresses and smiling at me through shiny glossed lips. Jasmine, the blond, was petite and tanned, a spray of brown freckles across her nose and between her breasts. Ryenne, several inches taller, was pale and more exotic, with dark, almond eyes and candy-apple red lipstick.

I know what you're thinking because I was thinking it, too. It was the potential realization of the standard heterosexual male's greatest fantasy. Here I was, in real life, acting out the lame, opening scene of a porn flick, lousy acting and all.

This is happening, I told myself, trying to behave as if having two hot strippers in my apartment late at night was a standard, every-day affair.

Just don't blow it.

I awkwardly offered them a seat on the couch, and I pulled up a cheap, folding chair for myself. As we sat there drinking, smoking, and giggling, I was only half paying attention to the conversation. There was another, infinitely more important conversation happening within my fevered brain, and it was with myself.

OK, how does this work? Who do I make a move on first? Should I come right out and suggest it? How do you pronounce it? Do I say "trois" with an "r" or a "w"? Do I pronounce the "s"? "Threesome" seems too crude. C'mon, man, you're smooth! You've got this! For the love of God, man, you're a musician!

Just as I was working up the courage to make my advance, an insidious seed of doubt wriggled into my brain, quickly sprouting and growing.

Wait. Oh, shit, I can't do this. I'm not one of those guys! Granny Johnson might be looking down at me and somehow get word to my mother. What if I can't perform? What if I over-perform? What if they both reject me at the same time? What if I'm totally misreading this entire situation? C'mon, Johnson, what are you waiting for?! Say something. Say something! DO SOMETHING!

It was too late. In horror, I realized the girls had lost interest. They had somehow detected my apprehension and deemed me an unworthy collaborator.

"OK, I think we're going to head out," Jasmine said. "Thanks for the company, Sweetie. We'll be at your show tomorrow night."

I'd hesitated, and my prey was moving off, out of range. The fantasy was fizzling before my very eyes.

Jasmine gave me a peck on the cheek, and Ryenne did the same. With slightly confused expressions, they shrugged and walked out into the night.

"Good night!" I called lamely after them. The door clicked shut.

Stumbling back, I collapsed into a fetal position on the couch, smacking myself on the side of the head like Chris Farley trying to interview Paul McCartney on *Saturday Night Live*.

"Stupid, stupid, STUPID! What did you just do?!"

I had come so close to living the dream, the Big Leagues of carnal pleasure, the T-Word. It was right there.

This became a seminal moment for me, one that would help to define the man I was becoming. After recovering from the initial devastation, I realized that my capacity for complete and total inhibition and rock 'n roll immorality did, in fact, have its limits. As much as I wanted to be Robert Plant, raging across 1970s America in a sex, booze, and drug-fueled Hammer of the Gods tour, it would never happen, no matter how famous I did or didn't become. I would always function as the person I was — Mark Johnson, youngest son of Hal and Sarah Johnson, from a North Carolina Christmas tree farm — whether I liked it or not.

I would have to leave the orgies to Led Zeppelin.

10

ART GECKO

Had I enough sense at the time to keep a journal, the following could've been the entry for Monday, January 23, 1995.

I awake to the rattling white noise of the decade-old, window-mounted air conditioner and try to focus on the red digital numbers of the clock radio. 6:55 am. Even this early, the tropical sun on the tin roof of The Mizzenmast is already generating more heat than the A/C unit can handle, and it whines in protest.

I roll out of bed with a moan, my head throbbing slightly, and my fingertips sore from four straight hours of guitar playing. Even though they each have thick calluses on the ends, my fingers require a period of recovery after every gig. Like most nights on the island, the last one ended much too late. Or early, if you're being technical. I got about three hours of sleep.

I brush my teeth and pull on my swim trunks, a clean t-shirt, and slip into my flops. I stuff a beach towel into my backpack along with the Larry McMurtry novel, *Pretty Boy Floyd*, a bottle of sunblock that I probably won't use, and my snorkeling gear, which I will. I grab a handful of one-dollar bills from last night's tip jar and stash them in the backpack, too.

After locking up, I make my way through the darkened office — the ladies won't arrive for another hour — down the steps of the defunct Mizzenmast Hotel, and into the courtyard where geckos skedaddle before me. There's a particularly big one that is always sunning himself on the same section of railing each morning, so I've named him "Art" as in "Art Gecko."

"Good morning, Art," I say. "Go eat the bugs in my room."

Art responds by licking his eyeball.

I use my key to open the wrought iron gate. Its squeak is the only sound on the street this morning.

I'm running a little late, so I double-time it down side streets to the Alley Galley market. It's the only place open this time of day where I can grab some breakfast for the boat. As usual, I purchase a cinnamon pastry and a bottle of apple juice. I'm in and out in less than a minute.

I continue down an unnamed path until it terminates at the harbor. My friend, Lisa, is opening her small jewelry shop as I walk past, so I slow down long enough to make a little small talk. But not much because, like I said, I'm running late.

"It's a hard life you have," Lisa says with a grin.

"It's a living," I reply with a wink.

I keep heading east along the boardwalk, passing the water taxi dock. Jimbo, the taxi captain, waves to me.

"Irie, Marcus!" he calls.

"Irie, Jimbo!" I yell back. "Don't forget to use your turn signals!"

My transportation for the day comes into view: the 42-foot catamaran Cutlass, the pride of Soggy Beard's charter fleet. Capt. Soggy Beard himself — or Ernest Alvarez, as he's known to his mother — is helping the guests aboard. There is a pile of shoes beside the gangplank because you go barefoot on the boat. I add my flops to the pile, wait until everyone else is on, and then it's my turn. I board the boat and find an empty seat among some 15 tourists.

7:45 a.m.

Ernest starts his speech. Nearly as tall as me, barrel-chested, and famous for his enormous salt-and-pepper beard, the boss strikes an imposing figure. He welcomes everyone, covers a few safety housekeeping items, makes a stale joke about falling overboard, and introduces the crew: Capt. Toussaint and his first mate, an amiable Marylander named Shea.

"We've got a special guest with us today, too," continues Ernest, his insane beard swaying sideways in the ocean breeze. "Mark Johnson, our Mizzenmast entertainer, is making the trip, so be sure to get to know him."

I wave to everyone and say hello.

Ernest has learned that its good business for me to go on this day trip to Buck Island because the people I meet will then come to see me play for the rest of their time in St. Croix. As you already know, Ernest owns both the charter business and the bar and intends to get every bit of value out of me that he can, which I'm perfectly fine with. It means I get to spend my day doing for free something that all these other people are paying good money for.

The boss says his goodbyes, steps off the boat and turns it over to Capt. Toussaint. The engine cranks and we motor off into the harbor, past Protestant Cay, and out into the Caribbean Sea, heading east. Though it's still early, the sun is already intense, and the scent of the air alternates between saltwater and Coppertone.

Time to inventory the passengers, as is my custom. All the tourists are Caucasian in various stages of sunburn, with a couple exceptions who are either already tanned or completely clothed. As a demographic, most appear to be in their 40s and 50s, and I can detect a mix of both American and European, perhaps Dutch and English, accents.

Suddenly, my focus narrows and mental alarms begin to sound.

A cute brunette in her early 20s, I figure, is on board and seated with an older couple. I assume these are her parents, so I study the situation for several minutes behind the relative safety of my mirrored sunglasses, pretending to read my book, head facing forward but eyes angled to the side.

She is slim, brown, and athletic with strong legs but slim ankles. She wears a white t-shirt tied at the waist and gym shorts over what I'm guessing is a swimsuit. Although the shirt is loose-fitting, it's clear as she adjusts her ponytail that she will do justice to her bikini top.

The girl affects an air of aloof royalty, aware of her status on the boat as the only young, good-looking female. Some of the older men are studiously trying not to look in her direction. Their wives make conversation with suspicious eyes, glancing toward the girl.

I bide my time, waiting for the right moment. I'm conscious of the fact that my long hippie hair and musician status might be a red flag for any father of an attractive daughter, but I'm armed with three secret weapons: my Southern accent, my background, and my manners.

As the Cutlass glides into the open sea, I begin introducing myself to the passengers, careful to start on the side opposite of the girl.

"I'm not an official crew member, but let me know if you have any questions," I offer to each group. "Capt. Toussaint and Shea might be too busy drinking rum to answer them."

It's a dumb joke, but dumb jokes often work.

Finally, I make it over to the family with the girl, affecting enough of my Appalachian drawl to be disarming but not off-putting. Where are y'all from, I ask. Texas, Dad says. Sounds like you're from the South yourself, he adds. Indeed I am, I say, having grown up on a Christmas tree farm in the North Carolina mountains.

Boom! The defenses drop. Dad now likes me, because how can you have a problem with a North Carolina mountain boy from a Christmas tree farm who says "yes, sir" and "no, sir"? I have secured my new, inner-circle status with Dan, Marie, and Chrissie from San Antonio. Chrissie is a University of Texas junior. She smiles a disinterested hello to me and turns her head to gaze somewhere else.

That's OK. I've got all day.

The trip is more than an hour from the dock to Buck Island, ranked by National Geographic as one of the world's top 10 most beautiful beaches. After several minutes of innocuous conversation with the Texans, I excuse myself back to my seat and open my book. Occasionally, I catch Chrissie peeking at me, but I don't react. It's still early in the day, early in the week, and I've got nothing but time.

THE TWIN PONTOONS OF THE CUTLASS CUT THROUGH the Caribbean Sea with ease, keeping the craft stable and level. No Dramamine is necessary on this boat, as opposed to a single-hulled craft that rocks from side to side, resulting in seasickness for many landlubbers. Not the Cutlass.

At the helm, Henry Toussaint — who usually goes by his last name alone — is the human representation of the Caribbean. He is eternally calm and is never flustered by anything that I can tell. Dressed in a light blue polo shirt, jeans, and a threadbare newsboy cap, Toussaint sprawls casually in the captain's chair, one hand on the tiller.

It's impossible to decipher the captain's age, mood, or anything else by looking at his face. Seriously, he could be 50 or

70. He could be currently joyous or mired in depression. Who the hell knows?

If the eyes are the gateway to the soul, Toussaint will remain a mystery. His small, dark eyes are nearly hidden in the folds of the blackest skin I've ever encountered. Even in bright sunlight, it's difficult to decipher the features of Toussaint's face, as if the reflective light is being swallowed by the pigment of his visage and placing him eternally in shadow. I don't exaggerate when I say this and I don't mean the description to be at all demeaning. To the contrary, Toussaint is, to me, a shadowy superhero, his superpower being complete and ultimate calm and the ability to project the same into any nearby person.

Originally from Aruba, Toussaint's language is barely English to the ears of a non-native. His dialect is so strong, he can be speaking to another Cruzan directly in front of tourists, and they won't catch a single word of it, as if he's speaking an altogether different language.

At first, I was a little scared of Toussaint, mainly because I couldn't tell what he thought of me. It was like spending the day with an expressionless black hole dressed in human clothing, and I made an incorrect assumption that he generally held me in disdain. But after a few days, I began to understand his dialect and mannerisms, and we developed a solid friendship after several long conversations.

"Ma-hk, how you doin' ta-day?" he would ask in his appropriately deep voice as we motored out of the harbor on the way to Buck Island. "I t'ink you had lot o' people at t'e Mizzenmast last night, ye'h? Girls, too, ye'h?"

One day, it dawned on me; Toussaint was a horndog — a ladies' man perpetually on the prowl. He would often quiz me on how many good-looking women had attended my show the previous night, and he had a debonair way of interacting with cute girls — most of whom could probably be his grandkids — on the boat. Knowing that few whites could understand him,

Toussaint was reckless and would openly discuss a woman directly in front of his subject. Rhonda told me that the captain once had a lurid conversation about her with another crewmember when she had only worked on the boat for a short while. She was standing nearly beside the two as Toussaint rambled.

"He didn't know that I had already deciphered the dialect, and he was having this very X-rated discussion about me," Rhonda laughed. "Finally, I just said, 'Toussaint, I understand you.' He jumped like he'd been stuck. He's been careful around me ever since."

Toussaint is also married, so I can't condone his behavior, though I'm certainly not one to judge. Honestly, I think he knows darned well that he has no real chance of scoring with 25-year-old white girls on vacation, so he just flirts to amuse himself.

9 AM.

We arrive at Buck Island and anchor offshore for snorkeling lessons. Shea distributes the snorkeling equipment to the tourists and gives them a quick tutorial.

"Is anyone concerned about snorkeling?" he asks.

A 60-something-year-old lady named Shirley, part of a group of chattering older women from Wisconsin, says she's never been and is nervous. I quickly volunteer to be her "buddy" and give her lessons.

"Ooo, baby, I've got me a musician!" Shirley yells to her cohorts. The boat erupts into laughter.

Meanwhile, Chrissie has stripped down to a minuscule blue-green string bikini. It's so small, it makes me uncomfortable on Dan's behalf.

I'm perfectly fine with it, though..

Time to get in the water.

I step off the stern of the catamaran and drop fins first into the Caribbean, swimming under the boat to where the ladder has been lowered and meet Shirley as she slips into the water with a squeal.

"You OK?" I ask.

"Yes!" she shouts back. "It was cooler than I expected!"

Chrissie now out of my mind, I take Shirley, a high school administrative assistant from Madison, through a short snorkeling tutorial. She's awkward at first, but pretty soon has the hang of it and begins to excitedly report what she is seeing every few minutes. One of the resident stingrays, nearly four feet across, glides directly underneath us.

"Blluuurrbbbb!" Shirley exclaims underwater, raising a cloud of bubbles, and startling the otherwise calm ray. It speeds away. I tap her shoulder and give her a thumbs-up, which she returns with enthusiasm.

Soon, the lessons are complete, and Shea blows a conch-shell horn as a signal to reconvene at the boat. We load back up and motor around to the east side of the island where the underwater trail is located.

The energy level on the Cutlass is now high as the newly trained snorkelers chatter about their lesson, adjust their mask straps, and slather on sunblock. I shoot a quick glance at Chrissie and see her bent over at the waist, head to one side, squeezing water out of her hair as young women do, acting as if they are completing some annoying chore but clearly putting on appearances for the male bystanders. When she glances up, I'm already looking the other way.

This game of cat and mouse can go both ways.

We anchor again over the deeper waters of the eastern side of Buck Island. Shea reminds the group to remove any shiny rings, as these have been known to attract barracuda, and we should aim to return this afternoon with all of our fingers. Eyes widen until the Marylander adds that this is just precautionary, and nothing to worry about.

"OK, you've got an hour here," he calls out. "Use the underwater markers to navigate through the trail. Stay with your buddy and above all, have fun."

Emboldened by her newfound prowess in the water, Shirley jumps in, giggling, and I follow. The two of us make our way through the trail, marked by various concrete placards on the seafloor. I point these out as we swim and Shirley responds with double thumbs up.

"Blluuurrbbbbb!" she says, again forgetting that her face is under water.

All manner of loudly festooned fish swim below us: blue tang, parrotfish, damselfish, angelfish, butterflyfish, trunkfish, puffers, you name it. Some move in great, synchronized clouds of purple, yellow, and blue. Others, like the spotted, wedge-shaped trunkfish, are solitary, exploring the ocean floor alone. Sunshine refracts through the crystal water, creating a chandelier effect that lights the ocean floor and its colorful inhabitants in a way impossible to imitate on land. Just yards away, the coral reef drops off and the water graduates into an impossible deep blue, the bottom somewhere far below.

Almost every day, I snorkel and dive into these waters, but it has yet to grow old; to the contrary, it never fails to amaze. It is an otherworldly, alien planet hiding in plain sight, daring us to look.

Predictably, Shirley is enchanted, nearly overwhelmed. As we tread water, heads above the surface, I explain to her how to dive and equalize the pressure in your head upon reaching a certain depth by pinching your nose and pushing air against your sinuses until your ears "squeak," and the discomfort disappears. I demonstrate this, diving some 25 feet to the ocean floor, propelled mostly by my fins. At the bottom, I look up at Shirley, wave, then do the classic "Walk Like an Egyptian" dance move. A massive cloud of bubbles erupts from Shirley's facemask.

We continue navigating through the trail. At one point, I glance to my right, out into the direction of the deep ocean, and spot a five-foot-long barracuda suspended motionless some 20 feet away, its silver-blue coloration making it nearly invisible. Even from this distance, I can clearly make out its gaping mouth filled with impressive, jagged teeth. I don't point this out to Shirley, but gently steer her in the opposite direction. Before we know it, Shea's conch shell horn is blowing.

We climb the rope ladder back into the boat as Shirley chatters and sputters. She is all smiles beneath a wet mass of silver-gray hair. "Thanks, buddy!" she exclaims as we make it onto the deck and wraps me in a bosomy hug. She announces to the boat in a loud voice that they should all go to my show tonight.

"Well, let me just say that Shirley will be my most badass audience member," I respond, speaking theatrically. "I just watched her back down a four-foot ray and a five-foot barracuda on her first snorkel ever. She never batted an eye. It was like diving with Clint Eastwood. Give it up for Shirley!"

The tourists erupt into cheers for my now-shocked buddy, who stares at me with wide eyes. "Holy buckets!" she yells before giving me a hearty high five.

I catch Chrissie peeking at me again. As we get underway, this time by sail instead of a motor, the Texan again wrings the Caribbean out of her hair with an aloof flourish and struts to the front of the catamaran, spreading a blanket over the netting that separates the two pontoons. She lies on her back in the classic sunbathing pose, placing her arms along her hips, one knee up, Ray-bans on, a whisp of dried salt across the top of her breasts.

I try not to notice. At least, not enough for anyone to notice me noticing.

The breeze fills our sails and pulls the boat toward the main island as Toussaint, reclined in the captain's chair, stoically tacks the Cutlass back and forth. People are tired but excited about telling their snorkeling stories to one another.

Out of nowhere, the wind dies as if shut off by some unseen switch. It's odd and a little disconcerting. The catamaran glides to a slow halt, floating perfectly still on a glassy ocean that is as calm as a pond. I can't get a clear answer from Toussaint, but this seems to be a localized variation of the doldrums, a phenomenon where prevailing ocean winds disappear suddenly. The doldrums have been known to strand sailboats for days, sometimes weeks on a motionless sea.

But since the Cutlass also has an engine, it's nothing to worry over, only an added, unexpected bonus for the passengers. I point out that we can look straight down into the water and clearly see a single starfish, the size of your hand, on the ocean floor 75 feet below. It's as if the still water is a gigantic reading glass, somehow magnifying the objects below and sharpening our own eyesight. Each of the starfish's five points is distinguishable.

The lack of wind in our ears is strange, and sound seems to be amplified as well, causing everyone to unconsciously lower their voices to near whispers. Each of us has become reverent, trying to absorb the grandeur and blessing of what we are all simultaneously experiencing. (Twenty-three years into the future, I would encounter similar surreal moments while hiking at 17,000 feet through the Himalayas.)

Toussaint starts the engine, and we begin motoring toward the St. Croix.

A HALF-HOUR LATER, WE'RE ANCHORED ABOUT 20 FEET offshore of the secluded Turtle Beach. The doldrums ended as abruptly as they began, and the winds are back to normal.

Serving as a de facto crewmember, I help Toussaint and Shea

carry several coolers through the surf to a narrow beach piled deep with pinkish sand. It's challenging to walk through the fine-powdered stuff with a heavy load, and this workout has me out of breath. The tourists follow through the waist-deep surf.

The Cutlass now empty, we lug the coolers into a picnic area cleared within a grove of palms and manchineel trees. Ever efficient, Toussaint lights charcoal in a grill and begins to arrange burgers, hot dogs, and chunks of fresh-caught grouper in his staging area. Shea is busy filling 10-gallon Igloo coolers with punch, then mixing in Cruzan rum. The activity attracts a mob of mongooses, materializing from the flora like little brown ghosts with wiggling noses that continuously test the air. This creates a stir among the tourists, and for the remainder of the lunch, these quirky creatures are the stars of the show.

Soon, the clearing is thick with the aroma of grilling foods. Now that the initial adrenaline of the snorkeling is gone and the wonder of the doldrums has subsided, the tourists realize they're famished, and everyone eats more than they planned. The teetotalers drink sodas and bottled water, but rum punch is clearly the favorite beverage.

1:30 PM.

"OK, everyone!" Toussaint shouts to the tourists who are seated in various places around the clearing. "Please put your messes in the trash bags and prepare to board 'd boat. Don't forget your sunglasses, your backpacks, or your husbands!"

It's a joke I hear almost every day, and although cheesy, it's not an unrealistic reminder. The rum punch began flowing about an hour ago, and the already happy moods of the tourists are now even happier if not downright jovial. It's not unusual for a sunburned landlubber, emboldened by the booze, to wander into the manchineel trees on a mission to catch a mongoose by hand, or something else equally stupid, and get turned around.

After everyone has been accounted for, the tourists stumble through the deep sand toward the anchored Cutlass. I help Toussaint and Shea load up the coolers, striding back and forth through the powerful surf. The waves on this end of the island are stronger, and the cool water feels good as it surges against my waist and stomach, repeatedly pushing me off balance. Before climbing aboard, I plunge underwater for one last cooling dip.

After Shea retrieves the anchor, Toussaint cranks the engines, shifts into reverse, and motors away from the private beach. Once safely in deep water, he shuts off the engines and raises the sails. The sheets billow with wind and we're propelled west toward Christiansted.

PLEASANTLY STUFFED ON HOT DOGS, HAMBURGERS, grouper sandwiches, and rum punch, the tourists find their places on the boat. Some, like my snorkeling buddy, Shirley, are still chattering about their underwater adventures. Others simply pass out under the shade of their straw hats or t-shirts draped across their faces. Shea produces yet another 10-gallon cooler of chilled libation, makes the announcement, and an eager line forms in an instant.

I enjoy this part of the trip. The hours exposed to an intense Caribbean sun and a cool salty breeze, the exertion of free-diving into clear, 80-degree waters, and the deceptively sweet alcohol create a slow-motion euphoria, and the world narrows to only the Cutlass and surrounding waters. The reality of commutes, deadlines, and staff meetings is a distant, slightly nagging memory for the adult tourists. Out here, without the responsibilities of the real world, senses are heightened, and inhibitions drop to nothing. Strangers this morning, the passengers now are old friends.

I get into a conversation with two 40-something fellows from Georgia, Gavin and Scott. They both work as manufacturers of plumbing fixtures and are visiting St. Croix as part of a business trip. Both are slightly overweight and have terrible sunburns that they are ignoring courtesy of repeated trips to the Igloo cooler.

After some general small talk, Gavin looks at me with slightly unfocused eyes.

"So, let me get this straight," he says. "They pay you to do this, correct? I mean, you're actually getting paid to come hang out on this island for two months?"

"Uh, yeah — that's pretty much it."

"And you're single," Scott adds as a clarification, more of a statement.

"Yeah, I've never really been in any one place long enough to have a relationship." I know what he's getting at, but I'm trying to keep everything G-rated.

The two men glance at each other, shaking their heads.

"I hope you realize that you're living out every guy's dream," Gavin says with complete sincerity. "No joke. You understand that, right? Brother, you've got it made."

I sit with his comment for several seconds, letting it cure. It would be pointless for me to mention what has led me to this gig. There's no way these two guys could understand the endless hours of practice, the dirty bars and empty venues, the indifferent patrons, or the drunken assholes who would insist on commandeering my microphone to shout offensive slurs at their equally inebriated friends. The countless cheap hotel rooms, the broken down or repossessed vehicles, the endless days of subjecting myself to door-to-door rejection, and the indifferent reactions from music producers and record executives — it would be meaningless. All of this would ruin the image for them, and I knew it.

"Yeah, I understand," I respond. "I'm one lucky guy."

I make a mental note that not a single day on this island will pass that I don't pinch myself and marvel at my surroundings. I'm not getting rich, nor am I any closer to my goal of having my music heard on a large scale, but it's OK. I am living life on a grand stage. It won't last forever, but it's happening now.

CHRISSIE IS SUNBATHING AGAIN ON THE FRONT netting of the Cutlass, and I brazenly join her since we're now old friends. We chat about a variety of meaningless things, topics that are exhausted by the end of each sentence. She giggles at my lame jokes from behind tortoiseshell Ray Bans, her smile crinkling a spray of brown freckles across her nose. Crystals of salt glitter like tiny diamonds on her skin. I realize that my eyes, bold from under the cover of my own mirrored shades, are lingering at her bikini top and I curse inwardly. Tourist girls vacationing with parents are off-limits, I remind myself. Off-limits!

It's an unspoken code among the locals. The young Americans and Europeans who staff the gift shops, jewelry stores, restaurants, and bars are fair game to each other — every night results in a multitude of fresh pairings — but the locals generally leave the tourists at arm's reach. It's bad for business otherwise.

I remind myself of these things, but the rum punch is making me reckless, and unspoken codes seem stupid and pointless.

3 PM.

Toussaint guides the Cutlass into its moorings where crewmembers tie it off to the deck cleats. The tourists off-load and begin searching through the pile of shoes for theirs, some of them stumbling as they bend over, giggling. Many either shake my hand or give me a bear hug, promising that they will attend my show tonight at The Mizzenmast. Chrissie neither hugs me nor shakes my hand. She simply smiles and waves, wiggling her tan fingers as she peeks over her shoulder. She and her parents soon disappear around the corner.

It's bad for business, I remind myself again.

As I walk back to The Mizzenmast, the streets of Christiansted are lively with cruise ship tourists loading up on duty-free liquor, jewelry, and other loot. As I reach the intersection of King Cross Street and Strand Street, I approach a beggar the locals refer to as "Quarter Man." At some point, he must have determined that soliciting quarters rather than some other denomination is most productive in his line of work, so every person that passes is met with, "Quarter? Got a quarter?" Quarter Man is tall and bony, has glassy, yellow eyes, and ancient dreadlocks. He is all Rasta and smells like 100-year-old weed.

As I walk past, he turns to me. "Quar..." He stops as soon as he recognizes me as the singer at The Mizzenmast. Some weeks ago, Quarter Man surmised that his daily income likely far outweighs mine and quit hitting me up for quarters. I am dismissed with a snort and a wave of his bony hand.

"Take it easy, Quarter Man," I say with a grin and flip-flop myself across the street.

It's five minutes later, and I've collapsed on my bed. I've got about five hours to nap, change my guitar strings, have dinner, and grab a shower before the patrons begin filling the chairs and barstools of my club. I try to fall asleep but can't. I'm tired but wired, nervous at the thought of my first song.

Will I remember the words to "Uncle John's Band" this time? Will my voice crack on the chorus of "Southern Cross," or will I miss the low note on "Handy Man" again? Will I recall the strange chord pattern of the bridge of "Rikki Don't Lose That Number" before it crumbles into a train wreck? I hope they don't ask for Dylan. Or Pink Floyd.

These are the same anxious thoughts that I have every day, about this time, six days a week. Today, I add another one.

Will Chrissie show up?

I shake off the notion and drift to sleep.

11

ONLY 20 DOLLARS

I t was a raucous night in The Mizzenmast.
A cruise ship had evidently docked for a couple of days in Frederiksted and had vomited a stampede of sunbroiled tourists onto St. Croix. Many had made their way to Christiansted along with a gaggle of early spring breakers fresh from the airport. As they were probably advised, the mainlanders avoided the more problematic areas of the town in favor of the relative safety of lower Queen Cross Street and had piled into my club with the enthusiasm of first-nighters.

It was early February, and I was now a veteran of more than 25 shows at The Mizzenmast. In many ways, I had morphed into a true islander, if not an honorary one. My hair was longer than ever, and a gold hoop earring shone in my ear. I had grown a goatee. My entire wardrobe consisted of three pairs of Levis cutoffs fringed on the edges by ragged white connective tissue, an assortment of faded T-shirts advertising various beers and liquors, a couple of swim trunks, and three sets of flip-flops. (I splurged on those.) My distant Cherokee blood seemed evident because I was as brown as a dermatologist's worst nightmare.

I had also become an official Christiansted street urchin. I knew practically every jewelry store and t-shirt shop owner in town. Nearly all the beggars, not just Quarter Man, had given up on asking me for money because they knew I was the "guitar mon" at The Mizzenmast, was part of the local economy, and was as insolvent as they. I could navigate the dangerous streets in the wee hours of the morning unmolested, though I usually carried a beer bottle or an oversized adjustable wrench I'd found in my apartment as a deterrent.

Tonight, The Mizzenmast was on fire. I was somewhere in the middle of my second set and it close to midnight — the shank of the evening in a town that was just getting warmed up. I was playing one upbeat cover tune after another — "Moondance," "The Joker," "Everybody Wants to Rule the World," "Sweet Home Alabama," "Brown-eyed Girl" — you know, crowd favorites. One song would lead directly into another as I relentlessly dissuaded the dancers from taking a rest. The dance floor was packed, mostly with University of South Carolina students reveling in an early Spring Break schedule. Now they were trying out their awkward reggae moves as I made my way through an acoustic version of Bob Marley's anthem, "One Love."

Several of the coeds remind me vaguely of Chrissie, the girl I'd met on the Cutlass nearly two weeks ago. Much to my disappointment, she never made an appearance at The Mizzenmast that night, and I could only assume she was back in Texas now. I wondered if things would've turned out differently had she been here with friends rather than her parents, but that mystery would go unsolved.

Thinking about Chrissie so distracted me that I didn't notice the guy until he was practically on top of me. It was Fati Master, one of the street Rastas who frequented the area and had evidently nicknamed himself in honor of a plump joint, although Fati himself was quite thin. He tended to lurk on street corners at night with his buddies, pushing weed on the spring-breaking college students. There were several Rastas who I liked immensely and was friends with, but Fati was not one of them. His condition was perpetually somewhere between bleary and unconscious, and he was humorless to the point of being flat-out rude. Plus, he never seemed to remember the fact that I wasn't interested in purchasing his product, which annoyed me.

Rastas rarely entered The Mizzenmast — they probably hated my music, and I didn't hold it against them — so it startled me when Fati appeared. He swayed at the front of the stage, directly before me, clearly trying to get my attention. As we made eye contact, he drew a fist out of his hoodie pocket and uncurled his fingers. I expected to see a crooked spliff, but instead, he brandished three sweaty, uncapped syringes in his cupped hand, inches from my bare knee. Behind him, the crowd swelled, bumping into each other, pushing him closer to me.

We stared at each other as I sang, and Fati began speaking to me, oblivious that I was singing.

"Only tweeny doh-lars," he was saying.

With my eyes, I tried desperately to convey the message, "Get the fuck away from me."

Fati swayed with glassy pink eyes, syringes jutting out between his fingers like an homage to "Wolverine" from The Avengers comics. I looked toward the bar for help. Rhonda was busy mixing drinks. Curtis, the bar back, wasn't even visible behind the crowd and wooden pillars. I had to do something myself.

For the first time in 10 years of playing in clubs, through hundreds of gigs and thousands of drunken fools, I did the unthinkable. I stopped. In the middle of a song.

"Quick break, y'all!" I shouted into the mike and grappled for the CD player beside me that was piped into the house system, starting a song before the crowd could realize something was up. I dropped my guitar into its stand, stepped off the stage, and grabbed Fati's bony elbow.

"Let's go outside," I shouted into his ear. "Put your hand back in your pocket."

We snaked through the humanity, a journey I thought would never end. Guys high-fived me and called out requests. A couple of cute coeds flashed their eyes at me — a gesture that would've customarily proved distracting in a positive way — but I hardly noticed. I pushed Fati through the crowd, holding the arm attached to his potentially fatal hand tight to his side, and I could feel him struggling to free himself. A possible scenario of him slashing out at the crowd — and me — with dirty needles infected with God-knows-what was enough to keep me focused.

We made it out the door, and I nearly dragged him down the steps to the street. Fati jerked his elbow away from my hand and stumbled, spinning to face me.

"Why you take me outta der like dat, mon? I know you gonna buy my sheet now! No white-ass bastard gonna fokin' disrespect me like dat."

Now, I've never been a violent kind of guy, and have usually avoided physical conflict at all costs. Simply being tall almost always kept me out of fights, which also meant I was inexperienced and could probably be dismantled with ease by a real fighter.

But this night, something in me snapped. My fear evaporated and was replaced with white-hot anger. In a quick step, I closed the distance between us until I was an inch from Fati's nose, looming over him with every bit of my 6'5" frame.

"Are you kidding me, you stupid motherfucker?" I hissed, channeling my inner Dirty Harry Callahan and spewing obscenities that I would rarely use in normal life. "You disrespect me by bringing that shit into my place of business. What you do out here is your own affair, but as long as I'm playing The Mizzen-mast, keep yourself and your goddamn stinking needles the hell out of there or you'll get more of this white-ass bastard than you can handle."

Fati's pink eyes widened, and he stared at me through his dirty dreds. In that instant, I figured I had a distinct reach advantage, not to mention the fact that he was hammered and I was stone sober. I calculated that I could take him, provided I could avoid the syringes. My hands balled into fists as adrenaline coursed wildly through my system.

Just then, a grin creased Fati's face. "Irie, mon," he mumbled and wandered off with a wave of his hand.

I stood there for a minute more until my knees buckled and I nearly fell. I crumpled to the curb, taking a while to compose myself before returning to the stage.

It was a late Sunday afternoon, several days after my near-fight experience with Fati, and I was hanging out in my apartment over The Mizzenmast. Sunday was my only day off of the week, and I had enjoyed most of it on a jet ski out at Buck Island with friends. Wind-burned and pleasantly exhausted, I had decided to spend the evening recharging for the next six nights of gigs and the inevitable after-parties. The streets were empty except for the occasional homeless person, and the shops were closed.

My apartment was not the kind of place where you would typically want to spend a lot of time. It was musty, dingy, and hot during sunny days, but not too bad at night.

Although comfortable, the vintage floral couch was nearly worn threadbare, with holes in the armrests and apple-sized discolorations in the fabric where dozens of greasy, throbbing, intoxicated heads had been propped over a couple decades. I'm not sure what color the carpet started out as, but now it was varying degrees of brownish-gray and, everywhere except under the couch, flattened in defiance of the most powerful of vacuum cleaners. Not that I had one.

Around the condenser part of the window A/C unit, a big white tumor of ice grew like an Arctic version of The Blob, requiring me to chip chunks of it off every few days lest it overtake the room. The walls were adorned with dusty, ancient hotel art and a rock-and-roll calendar from December 1990 featuring a photo of the band Mr. Mister. The concept of merely discarding the calendar never occurred to me, as it must not have for everyone else who had lived here since 1990.

Clearly, musicians don't give much thought to out-of-date calendars.

Even though the surroundings left a lot to be desired, it was occasionally preferable to remove myself from the everyday craziness and hole up with a book. I was munching on a bag of microwave popcorn, about halfway through my next Larry McMurtry novel, The Streets of Laredo, when I heard a strange noise.

Bump. Scrape.

It came from directly outside the apartment.

Reflexively, I glanced toward the bathroom just as the shadowed head of a human figure passed by that room's small window.

My face and neck went hot. The apartment was on the third floor of the building, so whoever was out there had climbed up and was walking on the roof along a narrow ledge not intended for people. There was no circumstance aside from maintenance that would've required someone to be on the roof, so I knew in a second that I was in trouble.

I rolled off the couch and hid behind it, spilling my popcorn in the process.

My heart pounded in my ears. Peeking over, I again saw the shadow pass by the window, which was mostly covered in a sheer curtain, heading in the other direction. The figure paused, I assumed, to try peering in.

Thud, thud, thud, went my heart.

I scanned the room to find a weapon and spotted my trusty adjustable wrench. The thing must've weighed two pounds and would have caused severe damage to an unlucky person on the receiving end of a blow. The handle was long enough that you could swing it like a ball bat.

I slithered over to the kitchen table, grabbed the wrench, and crawled toward the bathroom, not that crawling made any sense at all. I could hear footsteps and noises that suggested the intruder was checking for open windows on the office side.

My mind raced. I had absolutely no idea what I was going to do if the guy found a way into my apartment, aside from swinging at him with the wrench. If it found its mark, it could easily be fatal. Downtown Christiansted was empty and, as I mentioned before, the cops were reputed to be corrupt.

I was on my own.

The noises got slightly louder again. The prowler was heading back to my bathroom window, and by now, I was on the floor almost directly under it. I could see that the latch was unlocked and the sash was raised a couple inches. Do I jump up and slam it shut? My best shot at delivering a debilitating blow would be as the guy tried to crawl through the window. I froze.

Thud, thud, thud.

And then, he was right there. A dark hand reached under the sash and began to slide it up.

Now was the time, but in an instant, my plan changed.

I leaped toward the window and released the most powerful, guttural, ear-splitting, glass-shattering, Neanderthalic primal scream I could muster directly into the opening, unleashing the power of my professional-grade lungs to project my voice like some gothic banshee.

It delivered the desired effect.

The figure shrieked "JESUS!" and jerked backward toward the edge of the building as if he'd been electrocuted. His arms pin-wheeled wildly as he grabbed at the air and thrust his midsection forward in a futile attempt to retain his balance. In that millisecond, as the guy hung suspended in the air, I recognized the face.

It was Fati Master.

Our eyes met. If the world could have paused right then, we would have had this exchange:

Me: I had to do it.

Him: I know.

And then he dropped from my view, his long dreadlocks the last of him to disappear. What followed next was a cacophony of noise unlike anything I've experienced before or since. The closest description I can arrive at was the sound of Yosemite Sam, yelling nonsensical curses, bouncing down a long flight of stairs while wearing a suit of armor, having just swung at and missed Bugs Bunny with his Medieval sword. (Search "Yosemite Sam Cursing" on YouTube. It's hilarious.)

Crash! Bang! Clank! SHIT! Boom! Crash! Pow! FOOK!

Fati must have pin-balled from the tin roof of The Mizzenmast to the adjacent building on his way down to the alley, which contained numerous metal trash cans and a small dumpster.

CRASH!! A tomcat screeched — just like in the movies — and numerous dogs began barking somewhere down the street. The lid of a trashcan spun for a long time before clanking to the ground.

"Moothah FOOK!" The curse came from an obviously pained voice below, followed by a groan and what sounded like someone struggling through a jumble of debris.

That was it. Now I was on the offensive. Giant wrench in hand, I turned and raced through my room, out the apartment door, and collided with the corner of Julie's massive wooden desk in the darkened office, sending a cascade of papers, pencils, and ledgers flying through the room. I crashed to the floor, my head banging into a shredder machine. An angry knot immediately rose where my thigh had impacted the desk.

Leaping up with my own string of obscenities, I began a painful, limping descent down the steps, through the courtyard, and to the wrought-iron fence where I was again delayed by the process of digging the key out of my pocket.

Finally, I got the fence unlocked and rushed onto the street. I wasn't sure if I was finally going to be fighting Fati or performing CPR on him, God forbid, but by the time I got around the building and could see into the alley on the other side, he was gone. Several dozen CDs — including "Part of Me" by Mark Johnson — were scattered about the pavement along with a dinged up CD player, a shattered bottle of whiskey, and several drops of blood.

I lurched back into the street, grabbing at my leg and gasping for breath. A scraggly mutt trotted up the sidewalk, approached within 10 feet of me, and began barking repeatedly.

My thigh pulsing with pain, I reprised my primal yell.

"FUCK OFF!"

The dog yelped and ran away, tail between its legs.

RHONDA ARRIVED SOMETIME LATER, AND WE discovered that both The Mizzenmast and the first-floor clothing store had been ransacked, with Fati apparently forcing his way through a widow someone had forgotten to close. He managed to escape with a hundred bucks of petty cash.

I'm not sure it was worth the trouble, though.

A local ER nurse and Mizzenmast regular told me a few days later that a Rasta matching Fati's description had come into the emergency room late that same night. The guy was a mess, she said, with multiple cuts and bruises, and an ugly fracture of his right arm. He claimed he'd been in a car accident but refused to provide any details. After his arm was set and placed in a cast, the Rasta slipped out of the hospital and disappeared.

This closed the book on my feud with Fati. I didn't pursue anything with the cops, and I never saw him again. But from then on, it seemed that I had cemented a new status of respect among the Christiansted street Rastas.

"Gee-tah mon," they would say as I passed, raising a hand and tapping their chests. "Beeg lungs."

12

A GIG IN THE LIFE

Another entry in the journal I failed to keep...

I slip back onto the wooden stool to begin my second set. The cheap digital clock sitting atop my stack of PA gear reads 11:00 pm. A Sting CD plays over the house system, competing with the din of the murmuring and laughing crowd.

It's Thursday, February 16, 1995. As I adjust the mike and plug in my Takamine guitar, I scan the room.

Directly in front of the stage is the dance floor, probably 30 square feet of emptiness. Surrounding the floor are four-top wicker tables with matching chairs, all decades old. To my right is a long bar that has seen its better days and should've been replaced years ago. Beyond the dance floor, the wall facing the street is divided by two large entrance doors that lead onto a patio. Tonight, every available seat in The Mizzenmast is occupied, and many more patrons are standing, drinks in hand. The ever-popular patio is full as well.

Time to tune. I unplug my guitar cable from the BBE preamp and plug it into the small tuner perched on my knee. As I tune each string, making sure the indicator light on the tuner shines green before moving to the next, I scan the songs that are hand-written with Sharpie ink on two large pieces of white cardboard on the floor at my feet, mentally checking off the ones I've already played.

"Can you do any Jimmy Cliff?" a female voice shouts out.

I look up and catch the eye of the patron. I wink at her and mouth the words, "I can do one" while nodding, making a mental note to play "I Can See Clearly Now" later in the set. She grins, digs out a $5 bill, and trots up to the stage, depositing the money in the plastic drink pitcher with the word "Tips" written across it. I shout "Thank you!" to her as she scampers back to her seat.

I decide on the order of my first two songs: "Sister Golden Hair" by America and "One Particular Harbor" by Buffett.

"Sister Golden Hair" is perfect for launching a busy second set. The powerful opening guitar riff is so universally recogniz-able and loved, people will respond on a purely sensory level whether or not they actually like the entire song, and I want the energy to start high. It's a classic sing-along tune and shares its final chord, E, with the opening of "One Particular Harbor," creating a seamless transition that won't give the audience a chance to sit down.

It's funny the little things in life that make you happy. Simply knowing which two songs I'll play — and what the reac-tion from the audience will be — gives me a sense of private joy, as if I've got a wonderful surprise I'm getting ready to spring on a friend. I'm less than a minute away from unveiling this surprise, but the anticipation is nonetheless palpable.

The guitar now tuned, I plug back into the preamp, fade the Sting CD, and turn up the gain on the PA system. A couple of tongue clicks into the microphone confirms that it's hot, and I slide the volume on my guitar's onboard electronics up to the number I've chosen for strumming songs. (For quieter, finger-style songs, I go to a higher number.)

Faces in the crowd turn toward me, signaled by the absence of the house music. I look back at them and smile knowingly.

"Y'all ready?" I ask.

"YES!" comes a shout in unison.

I hit the opening chord — C-sharp-minor barred on the fourth fret for four beats — then A, four beats, then a booming open E, over eight beats. The low bass notes of the guitar blast out of the 16-inch sub-woofers of the hanging speakers, reverberating through the wooden structure of the room and into the very bones of the patrons. The riff takes about five seconds, but that's all that is needed. As one, the crowd, now an enthusiastic audience, turns to the stage and yells unintelligible words, holding their various drinks aloft. Girls pull their boyfriends and girlfriends toward the dance floor, nearly upending tables.

Ask any musician how it feels to command a room and you'll probably get various versions of the same answer. For me, it's a surge of adrenaline so powerful, I'm sometimes afraid it may topple me off my seat.

It's the understanding that the vibration of metal strings through a wooden instrument creates joy in other people, strangers, most of them.

It's the notion that air, forced by human lungs and passing over trembling vocal cords at precisely the correct rate and pressure to create notes in tune with the guitar and each other, has an emotional impact on others, sometimes moving them to tears.

This doesn't happen every night. Some shows fall flat and become wearisome, dreadful affairs. But when the magic is in the room, the feeling keeps you coming back, time and again, risking failure over and over. I liken it to a mediocre golfer who strikes a magnificent drive, a gift from the gods. All of those terrible slices and hooks immediately fade from memory.

The verse flows into the chorus, and now everyone in The Mizzenmast is singing along with the classic lyrics that were injected into the world's collective consciousness 20 years before.

By now, I know I've got them. It's just a matter of keeping them. As I sing, my eyes canvas the room. It's time to start making connections. Over there is a group of guys from Hess Oil. Behind them are Bill and Sue, an older couple I met earlier this week during a Cutlass trip to Buck Island. There's a gang of college students, not sure from where. Finally, my vision settles on a group of five women dancing to my left. They are in a circle, all holding a drink in one hand, laughing and singing. They appear to be in their late 20s or early 30s, and all are wearing what are, in my estimation, new outfits, undoubtedly purchased recently for some event. They dance with particular abandon, like sailors on shore leave.

Bridesmaids.

I make eye contact with one, a stunning brunette with long brown legs. The connection lasts just long enough to suggest something beyond mere friendliness. I glance at her left hand. No ring. She smiles shyly, which doesn't go unnoticed by her friends, who immediately start cackling and shouting at me.

"She likes you!" one yells, pointing directly at the brunette. "She wants to make out with you!"

The woman in question screams and dives behind her friends, mortified.

I grin as I sing, closing my eyes.

The song ends to thunderous applause, but I segue directly into "One Particular Harbor." Many in the room are clearly Jimmy Buffett fans, a.k.a. Parrotheads, and they recognize the opening sequence of chords immediately, rushing to the front of the stage. Thanks to the Caribbean-flavored rhythm, the rest of the audience remains on the dance floor, shifting into the much more seductive, Reggae-influenced tempo.

I begin singing the Tahitian opening phrases phonetically.

More cheers as the Parrotheads realize that I'm actually

performing the song correctly, not just winging it or mumbling through the foreign-language lyrics. Soon, the entire place is chanting the Tahitian refrain loudly (without knowing what it means), and I stop playing the guitar on a downbeat, switching over to handclaps, which is quickly taken up by the eager audience. Then it's back to the chorus and my thundering guitar.

Trust me, I understand that this isn't necessarily art. It's not music that will ever be vaunted by *Rolling Stone* magazine or studied in music theory classes. No, this is pure, unadulterated entertainment.

Some years ago, I came to terms with the contrasts between my day job — writing deep, meaningful music to feed my soul and creativity — and my night job — playing catchy, often shallow, sing-along songs for the enjoyment of rowdy, sunburned tourists. One job allows me to visit exotic locations and often pays well, while the other keeps me cooped up in shitty apartments and eating Ramen noodles.

I'm in "night job mode" right now, creating memories and stories for people I'll never see again and who will most likely forget my name by tomorrow morning. The fact is this: what I do is as valid as what any platinum-selling artist does; it's just on a much smaller scale and pays exponentially less.

I TRY TO BE REALISTIC ABOUT MYSELF AND PLAY TO MY strengths. I'm not the entertainer that many of my contemporaries are. Years ago, I decided that my shtick would be musicianship rather than stage presence, novelty sing-along songs, and cheesy humor (although I'll occasionally throw a little of that in.) Instead of comedy, I resolved to become a better solo guitarist than the other guys and to perform the cover songs accurately and with nuance.

Because I have a fairly utilitarian vocal range, this limited my choices. For example, I couldn't do many Dan Fogelberg or Kenny Loggins songs because of their insane vocal ranges. I would sound ridiculous trying to cover Queen, Led Zeppelin, Styx, REO Speedwagon, or any other band whose lead singer was a high tenor. Bob Seger was impossible. I was resolved not to make a fool out of myself nor to bastardize the song I was playing by dropping the key. (My only exceptions to this were the Eagles' "Hotel California" and "Take it to the Limit," both songs that I loved and was determined to do, even if I had to cheat a little.)

This is why I so connected with James Taylor. His vocal range was nearly identical to mine (though broader on both ends) and, because we were both raised in North Carolina, his pronunciation was equally similar. For some reason, I was able to mimic his unique style of guitar playing fairly well. JT's signature guitar sound developed because he had learned to finger certain chords "incorrectly," or in a non-conventional way — which informed the methods he used to transition from one to another — so nobody can *really* play James Taylor music true to form.

It was the same as how Hendrix and McCartney played right-handed guitars left-handed and upside down, or how Ringo played a conventional right-handed drum set-up left-handed. These little quirks were largely responsible for their uniqueness.

I also related to JT because we were both tall and thin — string beans, you could say — and this affected how we held the guitar and the tonal qualities of our voices.

Don't get me wrong. I could never aspire to the greatness of James Taylor nor did I seriously compare myself to him; it's just that I was able to cover his music in a more authentic way than, perhaps, others in my line of work.

I also decided early on that, unless I was playing with a band, my sound would be provided by my voice and guitar only — no drum machines, harmonizers, loops, or other gadgetry. I'd seen other players use these things, sometimes quite skillfully, but I wanted to travel light and deliver my music organically. I felt that if I could capture an audience without the electronic bells and whistles, I'd really have achieved something.

My electronics were only about delivering the best acoustic guitar and vocal sound possible. I wanted my audience to whisper to each other, "Man, this guy sounds great," rather than, "Man, this guy has cool gadgets and is really funny."

So did I succeed in my shtick of advanced musicianship? You'll have to ask someone else. Like any other purveyor of professional music, I played what made me happy, wrote the songs I wanted to hear, and sounded OK to myself, but it's impossible to objectively critique one's own art, if you want to call it that. I was certainly aware of when I played a song well and when I screwed it up, but that doesn't address how good the "good" really was.

All I know is that people kept paying me to do it.

THE NIGHT WEARS ON. I'VE KEPT THE NON-STOP, crowd-favorites coming relentlessly.

"American Pie," by Don McLean.

"Jack and Diane," by John Cougar Mellencamp (or whatever he was going by at the time.)

"Southern Cross" by Crosby, Stills & Nash.

"Lady Madonna" by the Beatles.

"Cool Change" by Little River Band.

The brunette bridesmaid is becoming bolder, pulling her friends over to dance directly in front of me and smiling seductively, no longer coy about her intentions. At one point, she drops a request, words scrawled on a napkin, into my tip jar along with some cash. Between songs, I fish it out.

"Feel Like Making Love!" the note reads. "For Dianna." As I

look at the feminine handwriting, I glance up and see her peering at me.

"Are you Dianna?" I ask into the microphone. She nods, now brave.

I smile, raise an eyebrow, and read the note aloud slowly, for effect. The crowd whoops in a conspiratorial tone, looking in her direction. Then, I look at her again.

"I do, too."

Cheers and laughs erupt, along with a chorus of exclamations from the bridesmaids as Dianna hides behind her hands, giggling.

With that, I'm off to the races again, playing the opening riff of the Bad Company song.

IT'S 12:30 AM — TIME FOR MY LAST BREAK.

"Folks, I'm going to take 15 minutes to grab a beer and take a breather," I announce to the audience, now even larger than before. "But stick around; the party goes until 2. Don't leave! You might miss something. And remember: Don't forget to tip your waitress and bartender."

I place my guitar in its stand, turn down both the microphone and guitar channels on the PA system, and start the house music. Stepping off the front of the stage, I make my way through the pulsing humanity, exchanging high-fives and fielding requests and accolades from the increasingly inebriated patrons.

Frank Foley grabs me as I slide through the crush of people.

"Hey, man, you sound great tonight," he says. "When things settle down a bit, how about 'Trying to Reason with Hurricane Season'? I could use a little poignancy tonight."

"You got it, buddy," I reply.

There's Toussaint, sitting at the bar. He merely gives me a

meaty thumbs up and smiles, gesturing at a willowy blond seated two chairs away. I shake my head at him as if to say, "Brother, that's nothing but trouble." He shrugs and takes a long pull on his bottle of beer.

I see more locals. There's Shea from the Cutlass and his ever-buoyant young wife, Stacy, who works at the desk in the Soggy Beard Adventures gift shop. They're chatting with Clay, one of my snorkeling buddies and a short-order cook. There's Lisa from the jewelry store with her husband, David, with whom I jet-skied before sending Fati Master to the hospital two weeks ago. There's Laura, a tall, slim brunette with a Dorothy Hamill haircut, a clerk at a different jewelry store. She and I have been flirting relentlessly for weeks, but the stars have yet to align. From behind the bar, Rhonda catches my eye. Without a word, she pops the cap off a sweaty bottle of Dos Equis Mexican beer, jabs a slice of lime onto the rim, and sends it to me through the crowd via assembly line.

Taking my beer, I step through a hanging tapestry that covers a darkened back hallway, not meant for patrons. I find the tiny employee bathroom and freshen up, splashing cold water on my face. The bass line of "Run Around" by Blues Traveler rattles the mirror in the bathroom, barely illuminated by a single 40-watt light bulb. I step out and turn right in search of fresh air, following the walkway that overlooks the old hotel courtyard. As I move out into the night, I detect a presence following me and turn to face whoever it is, gripping the Dos Equis bottle like a possible weapon.

It's Dianna, the brunette with brown legs.

"Hi," she purrs. Before I can respond, she pushes me against the wall, closing her mouth over mine. She tastes like spearmint gum with a hint of Cruzan rum.

That's a good thing.

It's 12:50 AM.

I'm five minutes later than I expected in returning to the stage.

As before, I choose my opening three songs from the cardboard setlist while tuning my guitar. I'm finding it difficult to concentrate, to think straight.

C'mon, man.

Get the girl out of your head. Be a professional.

I settle on "Son of a Son of a Sailor" to open, followed by Van Morrison's "Brown Eyed Girl." Rhonda had earlier given me a Mizzenmast t-shirt to use as a giveaway, so I'll quiz the audience with the third song, "Something About You" by Level 42. Whoever correctly names the band first gets the shirt. (They always think it's Tears for Fears.)

The plan is flawless and by the end of "Something About You," the entire room is singing the chorus in unison.

As I hit the last line, I glance at Dianna, who is singing the lyrics pointedly back to me.

Concentrate.

Some twenty minutes later, I notice one of the local beggars walk in. Veering, he grabs an empty chair, drags it to the center of the dance floor, and sits facing me with his arms crossed. A five-foot radius quickly forms around him, with patrons staring. With bleary eyes, the guy — I think his name is Freddie — pulls out a crooked joint and fires up. He shows no sign of enjoyment of the music at all, only stares and sucks on the joint.

These guys know they're not allowed in the bars, but will occasionally test the system out of boredom, I suspect. I glance across the room and can see that Rhonda is talking with Curtis, the bouncer, and formulating a plan. I doubt she will involve the big guy, though. A brawl on the dance floor would be dangerous and terrible for business.

The waitress, Amy, says something to Freddie, but he seems to ignore her. The dance floor is now empty save for the beggar, arms crossed, staring at me. In a vain effort to defuse the tension, I sing the classic Marley song of peace and inclusiveness, "One Love." Freddie, however, is unmoved, literally and figuratively.

Suddenly, Rhonda appears and approaches the beggar. She speaks into his ear and motions toward the front entrance, smiling and flipping her sun-bleached hair. With a look of sudden interest, he stands up, wobbles, regains his balance, and follows Rhonda out the entrance and down the steps. After a minute or two, Rhonda reappears without Freddie to raucous applause, with patrons spilling back onto the dance floor.

Rhonda told me later that she propositioned Freddie and invited him to "go somewhere" with her. In his weed-induced state of over-confidence, he agreed. When they walked out, she had a taxi waiting on the street in front of the bar.

"You first, big boy," Rhonda had intoned, giving Freddie her best Mae West impersonation.

After he slid into the back seat, Rhonda slammed the door and yelled at the driver to take off, tossing a $10 bill into the front seat. The rusty little taxi sped away, disappearing around the corner with the Freddie cursing out the window. It was a stroke of genius and the type of quick, critical thinking Rhonda was known for. She solved the problem without any violence at all.

It's 1:50 AM.

Most of the crowd has dispersed, but there are still some 30 patrons in The Mizzenmast. I'm closing out the evening with three songs designed to send people home happy and spent, either alone, with a significant other, or in a new, lustful pairing. Last up is Frank's Jimmy Buffett request, "Trying to Reason with Hurricane Season," an extended, obscenity-laden version of

James Taylor's "Steamroller Blues," which whips the crowd into a frenzy, and finally, a poignant "Take it to the Limit" by the Eagles.

"Thank you very much for hanging with me tonight!" I say over the whoops and applause from the audience as I end the Eagles song with a flourish. "Enjoy the rest of your stay on St. Croix. Goodnight!"

Down go the microphone and guitar channels on the PA system, up goes the house music, this time at a much lower volume. As one, the crowd begins milling out and down the steps. I glance to my left. Of the bridesmaids, only Dianna is left at the table. I can see that she has reapplied her lipstick and is chewing gum. She shoots me a dazzling smile, mouthing the words, "Hurry up."

I look to my right and see Toussaint, still in the exact same position at the bar, smirking at me. With a tip of his head, he gestures to Dianna as if to say, "Brother, that's nothing but trouble."

I smile back at him with an exaggerated shrug.

Once more into the breach, Toussaint.

13

HOGS AND BOATS

As landmasses go, St. Croix is small. It's 22 miles long and 7 wide for a grand total of only 82 square miles. For the sake of comparison, St. Thomas is 32 square miles, Puerto Rico is 3,515, and Tennessee is 14,143.

Santa Cruz, as Columbus first referred to it, looks lonely on a map. It sits by itself almost 70 miles away from the other U.S. and British Virgin Islands — St. Thomas, St. John, Tortola, Virgin Gorda, Anegada, and Jost Van Dyke — which are literally next door to each other and all having a gay old time. St. Croix is like the slightly chubby kid from the wrong side of the tracks that nobody wants to play with.

This probably explains why the island was favored by the worst of the pirates and rulers of the 17th and 18th centuries while also coveted as a getaway for well-to-do Europeans. There's no question about it: When you're on St. Croix, you are most undoubtedly isolated.

It's also remarkable that in only 82 square miles, St. Croix manages to support several distinct ecosystems. The east end of the island, which, at Point Udall, is generally recognized as the easternmost spot of the United States, has an arid, desert climate, while the hilly western side is lush, green, and boasts its own rain forest. It's as if God felt a little guilty about plopping the island all the way down there by itself, so he decided to spice things up a bit by letting it have its own ridiculously varied weather. I'm no climatologist, but I can't imagine that 82 square miles anywhere else in the world can make such a claim.

Even though the island is sublime in all the ways I just mentioned, I didn't explore very much of it for a very practical reason: I didn't have a car. Plus, there was the fact that people drove on the left side of the road, which terrified me. There were times when Rhonda offered to let me borrow her truck, but I quickly declined for fear that my brain would short-circuit while trying to both navigate through unfamiliar territory and drive like an Englishman, and I would crash and kill myself. As a result of this apprehension, I simply walked my laundry to a nearby laundromat, bought my meager groceries from the Alley Galley, and ate out almost every day.

There were occasions when I tagged along with someone else to restaurants and other establishments outside of Christiansted. On one such trip, with Rhonda, Frank Foley, and a couple other folks, I was introduced to the (now-famous) beer-drinking pigs that I had seen the sign for on the trip from the airport. We were bound for a Sunday evening Reggae festival in Frederiksted but detoured onto a winding road that took us through the rain forest to Mt. Pellier Domino Club.

"You can't come to St. Croix and not see the beer-drinking pigs," Rhonda stated matter-of-factly as we pulled into the parking area. I didn't argue.

The bar was situated right alongside the road and looked like something out of "Swiss Family Robinson." It was a surprisingly large structure, the sides of which were constructed of bamboo, the roof of thatch. Inside was a bar and plenty of four-top tables with plastic chairs. A bosomy, heavyset black lady immediately greeted us with a wide smile.

"Welcome to Mt. Pellier Domino Club," she said with a sing-songy Cruzan accent. "My name is Norma. Can I start you out with a 'Mama Wanna' today?"

I looked at Rhonda and shrugged.

"Absolutely, bring us all one," Rhonda said. "Thank you, Norma."

By this time, I had mostly given myself over to whatever people, especially Rhonda, told me to do and try, so I was anxious to sample a Mama Wanna. I wasn't disappointed. Norma mentioned that the ingredients were secret, but after much consternation, our party was able to deconstruct the drink, figuring it contained rum, honey, and various other spices that have since escaped me. When we brazenly confronted Norma with this information, she simply smiled.

"You can t'ink what you t'ink," she said with a hearty laugh, omitting the h's as Cruzans tend to do. "I'll never tell!"

As much as I enjoyed the drinks, I was here to witness some beer-drinking pigs and not to get drunk on Norma's classified brew, and I said as much. In retrospect, I can see that the pig part of the experience was only improved by mild inebriation, which is probably why the tour began in the bar and ended at the pigs, not the other way around. We paid Norma a few bucks, and she handed over a six-pack of O'Doul's non-alcoholic beer.

"If I were one of these pigs, I'd hold out for a proper beer," Frank commented.

The animals were housed in a covered, concrete stable of sorts just up the hill from the bar. When I finally got a look at the two pigs, I was shocked. I had pictured a gang of cute, pink, Charlotte's Web-type creatures, perhaps sitting upright around a small table and wearing hats, toasting each other with tankards of brew held carefully in cloven hooves.

Not hardly.

These were massive hairy hogs, one entirely brown and the

other, a splotched white and tan. They snorted at us with ghastly pig smiles.

"This is how you do it," said an unimpressed Frank Foley. He approached the waist-high wall of one of the stalls and tapped his can of beer on the top. The brown hog within immediately sprung up onto its hindquarters with its front legs resting on the wall, its hooves dangling casually over, like your backyard neighbor leaning against a fence to have a chat. Its mouth gaped open menacingly, exposing two fang teeth. Frank simply dropped the unopened can into the thing's mouth.

WTF? was my immediate thought.

Eyes half-closed in apparent ecstasy, the pig began crushing the can in its great jaws like a crocodile chomping the femur of a wildebeest. White foam sprayed out in all directions as he munched on the unfortunate vessel, gulping down the liquid. The remains of the can were then unceremoniously spewed onto the floor along with several other aluminum carcasses. The entire process took about 15 seconds, after which the hog was clearly ready for another, still draped over the wall, smiling. I walked up, deposited my can into the gaping maw, and the madness was repeated.

The pigs didn't so much drink the beer as they mangled it, but I guess the phrase "beer-mangling pigs" wouldn't play as well on the signage.

I stood in a lush tropical rainforest, the songs of exotic birds echoing through the vegetation, interrupted only by the screeching, metallic din of the O'Doul's beer can being destroyed by the maniacal jaws of a gigantic, grunting hog.

"Clank!" went the remains, spat onto the concrete beside my foot.

I turned to Rhonda.

"Okay, I'm good."

∿

I WAS NEVER A BOAT PERSON UNLESS YOU COUNT canoes, and even then, it was rare. The vast majority of the time I spent interacting with water as a kid was fishing in the New River of Ashe County, North Carolina, for redeye, hornyhead, and smallmouth bass, while wading through the cool, shallow waters in whatever battered sneakers had finally been retired from active service on dry land. In my narrow view, boating was an expensive and unnecessary complication.

In college, I became a decent body-surfer off the beaches of the Outer Banks, particularly the island of Ocracoke, but again, this didn't involve a boat. Sure, a boat was required to reach Ocracoke — a ferry, to be exact — but once there, I reverted to a typical dry-lander making lame attempts to appear confident in the foamy green Atlantic surf. The idea of boating in the ocean was as strange to me as boating anywhere else.

In the islands, though, everyone has a boat. It's just a given.

If Saturday nights were dedicated to drinking to excess and celebrating life in The Mizzenmast, Sunday afternoons were for … well … doing more of the same. Only now, the celebrations moved to a floating collection of wood and fiberglass. After a few meager hours of sleep, locals would load their alcohol and food onto their craft and sail or motor out to the western side of Buck Island.

I experienced this one Sunday afternoon, the date of which escapes me, as well as the name of the person who took me. It could've been any number of people because A) everybody had a boat, and B) people were constantly abducting me. Sometimes these were young women with ulterior motives. Sometimes they were older, matronly women who felt the need to mother me. One appealed to Dr. Jekyll, the other to Mr. Hyde, but in either case, I was usually game. More often than not, though, I was just a member of the gang of Mizzenmast regulars, another person to help carry a cooler.

Somehow, this particular day, I ended up on a sailboat in a

cluster of some 50 others that were anchored off Buck Island in the same waters where the Cutlass would stop for snorkeling lessons. This was the St. Croix equivalent of the Saturday night "cruising" of my youth, when the main drag of West Jefferson would be lined with the newly washed and waxed vehicles of every high schooler in Ashe County. (We would slowly drive past one another for hours, hoping for the courage to actually arrange a rendezvous with an adequate member of the opposite sex. If successfully organized, the awkward grope session frequently took place between the tall stacks of wood pallets at a nearby sawmill.)

At Buck Island, the surroundings were decidedly more exotic, if not dangerous, due to the fact that we were all drinking and swimming — not a brilliant combination. Revelers visited each other's craft by simply swimming between them, and I'm sure that the continuous plunging into the water by Coppertone-slathered bodies created an oil slick in the vicinity of Buck Island that would've been visible by air. The intermingling of multiple boom-boxes, laughing voices, and bodies plunging into the water created a cacophony that reverberated off the sides of the vessels.

At one point, I found myself aboard a sleek schooner owned by a clearly well-off couple from Martha's Vineyard. Soon after I climbed aboard and was introduced as The Mizzenmast musician, the man disappeared into his galley and returned with — you guessed it — a guitar. For the next hour, I entertained his passengers along with those on another 10 or so boats that had quickly surrounded the schooner and anchored. Predictably, the impromptu gig consisted mostly of Jimmy Buffett music. (Their names forever lost to my faulty memory, the boat owners would appear later that week at The Mizzenmast, dropping two $100 bills into my tip jar with a note that read "Thanks again!")

As dusk began to settle over St. Croix, the boats dwindled down to just a few and the sounds quieted, so I decided to take a little time for myself. I said my goodbyes to the owners of the schooner, dove off the boat, and swam the short distance to Buck Island, collapsing onto the pinkish-white sand in a sort of satisfied, exhausted, and mildly drunk ecstasy. My feet dangled in the docile water and tiny minnows clouded around my toes, nibbling at whatever appealed to them in the browned skin of my digits. It tickled, and I had to concentrate not to jerk my feet away.

Propped on my elbows, I gazed across the preposterous beauty, trying to absorb the scene. Suddenly, the three masts of the schooner illuminated with a string of white Christmas lights. The triangles glimmered in all directions, reflecting off the ocean's surface as the sun, now a dark orange globe, dropped into the Western horizon. For a moment, I wasn't sure if this was reality and not either déjà vu from a past existence or the fertile imagination of a 13-year-old farm kid in a barn. After convincing myself that the moment was actually happening, I made a conscious decision to commit it to memory.

"Remember this," I said aloud, wiggling my toes at the cloud of hungry minnows. "Remember this."

14

MISFIRE

Tuesday, February 21, 9:25 am.

A steady rain dances across the tin roof of The Mizzenmast's third-floor office/apartment. Combined with the incessant drone of the air-conditioner, the resulting white noise is almost overpowering, but also pleasing.

Most afternoons, a warm Caribbean shower washes the streets and rooftops of Christiansted, lasting only around 15 minutes before the sun overtakes the clouds with renewed vigor and dries everything out once again. But today, a rare, low-pressure system has decided to linger over the entire island, topping off thousands of rooftop cisterns with life-giving fresh water to the delight of everyone except the boat operators and beach vendors. They will make no money today. At least not for a few hours.

For me, the rain is an excuse for learning a new cover song or two, reading in the comfort of air-conditioned shade rather than on a sun-beaten catamaran, and making phone calls home.

Adding a new song is not as easy as it may sound. It is a matter of situating myself on a sunken couch, boom-box on the coffee table, and re-playing a cassette tape over and over again, trying to decipher that one chord that befuddles my brain or that line of lyric that is unintelligible and/or makes no sense. Beside me sits a battered notebook and a pencil. I write the lyrics and chord changes in sloppy cursive, hoping I can read them later.

Dammit, Elton John! Speak clearly!

It can't be "learning Alta's muse 'sup fear a bone."

Or, "turning out his views pup mere atones."

Okay, I'm going with "burning out his fuse up here alone."

If only there were some type of readily accessible library, something I could get to without leaving the apartment, where I could quickly find lyrics displayed neatly in easy-to-read type. Maybe I could even find the chord changes this way, too! Ah, but I dream. Little do I know that within 15 years, deciphering chords and lyrics will be as simple and magical as tapping the glass cover of a wallet-sized rectangle held in the palm of my hand.

But this is 1995, and that's just crazy talk.

Click, whirl, click, whirl, click, whirl, goes the boom box cassette player.

Two hours later, I feel 95-percent sure I have it, which is good because I've twice had to re-spool the tape onto the cassette's rollers using my trusty pencil, a tried and true method used by anyone in my general age demographic. A CD player would've been nice, but that would be too much to ask of this ancient apartment.

Now, I will practice "Rocket Man" for 60 minutes straight, obsessively finishing the song and then starting back at the beginning. Tonight, I will work it into the set somewhere near the beginning, while people are still mostly concerned with conversation and aren't paying close attention. After the first public performance, I usually have the song committed to memory and add it to my cardboard setlist.

12:30 PM.

I hang up the phone and sigh. My Nashville publisher, Reggie, had nothing exciting to report. He has pitched several of my songs over the past month to artist & repertoire (A&R) reps from Capitol Records and Arista Records, as well as multiple producers. A couple of the songs were put on hold, Reggie said, but I know this means practically nothing. Meanwhile, the company has been recording more demos with several of my fellow songwriters — all of whom write conventional and commercial country music — and I know that Reggie will push these over my older, left-of-center, folk-rock songs. Out of sight, out of mind.

I'll admit it. Working in the music industry has made me cynical to the point that I'm unfazed by almost anything. I've met with famous producers, publishers, songwriters, and platinum-selling artists. Last year, I even drove to Los Angeles to visit with a Capitol Records executive in the company's iconic round skyscraper, the one that resembles a giant stack of dinner plates. It had taken three days for me to drive a borrowed minivan across the country, and the meeting lasted all of 10 minutes.

"Hmm," the executive, dressed in all black, had said as he listened to the first few seconds of my CD. "I'll let my colleagues hear this when I get a chance. Thanks for dropping by." He stood up and held his hand out.

My first inclination was to strangle the guy, but I rose from the chair and forced a smile.

"Yeah, it was no problem," I said, shaking his hand, squeezing it a little too hard. "I enjoy dropping by places that are 2,000 miles away. I may pop into London next week. Or, perhaps, Alaska."

Never heard from that guy again, to no one's surprise.

But that was only one example of many. The past five years had been a series of "exciting possibilities" followed by the inevitable let down.

You're great, but not quite right for Record Label XYZ.

The song is great, but not quite right for Artist XYZ.

The life of a musician on the cusp of success is the ultimate Catch-22. You are expected to produce reams of new songs, record libraries of demos, and keep your live performance chops up, all while somehow paying the same bills as a person with a conventional, full-time career. It's nearly impossible to have a well-paying, non-music job while fully pursuing the business. This usually equates to living in squalor in Nashville — washing dishes or selling frozen meat — or traveling away from where you should be to play other people's music, as I'm doing now.

It's sometimes a little tough to stay upbeat. Oh, don't get me wrong — I know how it appears to a person with a real, 9-to-5 job: I'm living in the Caribbean, supporting myself by nothing more than singing and playing guitar, and enjoying a nightlife that would make Caligula mildly envious. I can't argue with the image of it. But a nagging feeling that has followed me like a loyal cocker spaniel for the past decade keeps rearing its head.

Is this all there is?

I can't buy into the concept that I was placed on this Earth to simply regurgitate other people's art, even if I'm pretty good at it. But trying to break through that invisible ceiling of success in the real music business — y' know, the one where you're making ends meet by playing your own songs — seems as likely as climbing Mt. Everest and I'm not sure if I'm equal to the job. I don't know that I was created to be a hit songwriter or a famous pop star, even if Lady Luck were to put me there. And playing six nights per week at a time-weathered St. Croix tavern feels like some insignificant fuel stop on a much greater journey.

It's good that these rainy, contemplative days don't happen often. On the boat, or 15 feet underwater, I'm usually too distracted by bikini-clad women and schools of purple tang to fully engage in such dark introspection.

The apartment suddenly feels like it's closing in on me. A glance out the window confirms what the lack of noise from the roof suggested — that the rains have stopped. I grab my backpack, step into my sandals, and head out, desperate to clear my head.

I decide to visit the bright yellow and white Fort Christiansværn, not even a 10-minute stroll east down Company Street. I pay a small entrance fee and walk in among a few scattered tourists and school children.

Framed against an impossibly blue Caribbean sky strewn with cheerful white clouds, the bright, summer-sweet-corn hue of the Danish structure is made even more so, almost painful to behold. A gentle, 78-degree breeze swirls through the various open archways, windows, and halls, and across a Bermudagrass lawn, manicured like a putting green. Just inside the first doorway, a commemorative plaque is affixed to the wall. It reads:

Fort Christiansværn

1738

Built on the site of earlier French earthworks, this Danish fort guarded town and harbor through the perilous early years. The mission was accomplished: attack never came. Later, as police station and court, Christiansværn continued in the cause of peace.

There are very few American structures that date back as far as this, a fact that isn't lost on me. I make my way through a variety of historical displays, past barracks and dungeon cells, and up onto the roof where a battery of six impressive cannons face Christiansted Harbor. There is something incongruous in the sight of these menacing weapons pointed directly at a flotilla of sailboats and pleasure craft bobbing quite peacefully in the clear waters of a tourist town. I wonder if some of the native Cruzans are ever tempted to sneak up here after hours and set these things off, obliterating as many sailboats as possible as revenge for past injustices. It's easy to picture.

Dreadlocked Cruzan, as he touches the tip of a lit joint to a cannon's fuse: This is for Great-Great-Great-Great-Great-Great-Uncle Leo!

Cannon: BOOM!

Dreadlocked Cruzan: That was cool. Okay, who's got more weed?

Frankly, I'm amazed that very scenario has never happened.

I shake the thought out of my head. It's hard to fathom that I'm standing within the same brick and mortar that was placed here by slaves 257 years earlier, back when America was still four decades away from proclaiming its independence and pirates still roamed these waters. It makes me wonder who the 1738 equivalent of me was, and what were his challenges.

Most historians agree that musicians were held in high esteem in the 17th and 18th centuries, particularly aboard pirate vessels, where life was boring more often than not. Just the thought makes me feel for those guys. I can picture the poor performer trying to get through some really poignant, original fiddle tune while drunken crew members yell, "Blow the Man Down!" from the back of the room. (This undoubtedly was to the pirate musician what "Free Bird" is to me. Or perhaps, "Margaritaville." Only I'm not usually made to walk a plank if I choose not to play it.)

In all seriousness, the sheer existence of the fort only serves to reinforce my earlier feelings of self-doubt. Once, the people who settled here were so concerned about their safety that they constructed a military fort to protect themselves, and they had good reason. The prior 200 years had been filled with murder, conquest, and enslavement. The sheer brutality of several of the pirates who frequented the area was unthinkable. Take, for example, the French buccaneer Daniel Montbars, known as Montbars the Exterminator. According to historian David Cordingly, Montbars' favorite method of killing enemy soldiers — possibly right here on St. Croix — was to cut open their stomachs and nail their large intestines to a wood post. As if that wasn't rude enough, he would also make them dance by beating the hell out of them with a burning log. (Think about that. A *plain* log didn't do the trick for this guy. It had to be on fire.)

In contrast, my main worry is correctly interpreting Elton John, and if I get it wrong, no one will notice.

So imagine being the entertainer who was charged with keeping a homicidal maniac like Daniel Montbars happy. The man's very life may have relied on his ability to temporarily undo the boredom and depression or even murderous rages of others. I wonder if he had some of the same thoughts as I.

Is this all there is?

THAT NIGHT TURNED OUT TO BE A GREAT EXAMPLE OF a bad gig. The unusual steady rain that returned after my visit to the fort had dampened more than just the rooftops of St. Croix; it also had clearly ruined the party atmosphere of the entire island. The Mizzenmast morphed into one of the many dreary venues that I had played in the past, with only a smattering of indifferent, apathetic patrons.

Being a soloist has its perils. You not only enjoy 100 percent of the accolades on a great night, but you expose yourself to 100 percent of the mortification on a terrible one. A bad night for a band is entirely different. It becomes fodder for jokes and silliness, and you begin to play to each other. Sometimes, it's just a paid rehearsal, but regardless, you have your band-mates beside you for empathy, and the gig simply becomes another story you can laugh about in the van later.

A soloist enjoys no such support.

Performing music alone for a listless, unenthusiastic audience is one of humankind's most soul-crushing experiences. There's just nothing quite like it. You wonder if the people would rather you just weren't there at all, and the silence at the end of each song is overpowering.

To this end, there were various methods I used to try — unsuccessfully — offsetting the mortification. For example, I would run each song into the next without pause — one after another for 90 minutes — just to eliminate the opportunity for embarrassing silence. This was Method #1. If that failed, I would simply play the music to songs without singing at all, or worse yet, invent instrumentals on the spot. This resulted in me coming off more like a background musician than the actual entertainment, making the apathy of the room easier to swallow. In other words, I acted as if I didn't expect to receive applause, so if I did, I'd respond with a surprised comment.

"Oh, wow," I'd say into the mike. "Thanks. I really appreciate that."

After an hour or two, things might get weird. Sometimes, I would make up a fictional friend who had entered the back of the venue, and gesture to him during the song, as if I was excited to see my buddy. At the end of a set, I'd push the microphone away, gesture to my "friend," and mouth silent words.

"Hey, man! Hang on a sec. Am I going back there or are you coming here? Okay, cool, just a sec," I'd silently say across the room to my invisible friend. The idea was, this would relieve the obvious embarrassment of a friendless loser trying unsuccessfully to entertain a smattering of uninterested people. The real insanity was, I doubt that the audience ever actually saw me doing this, so the ruse was moot, and I sat there having a conversation with an imaginary friend by myself.

We've all experienced slow-moving time in our lives. A boring class in college or high school, for example. Sitting through a long-winded church sermon when you're 15 years old. Attending a two-hour insurance seminar on a Tuesday morning.

But trust me, none of this compares to the agony of playing a four-hour solo gig for a shitty audience. The rules of time and space in that particular location on Earth alter inexplicably until the hands of the clock move at roughly the speed of an elderly sloth. You lose all focus on the flow of the set as what little adrenaline your body created at the outset of the gig drains out the ends of your toes. You are now playing at people rather than for them, looking out at the back of heads rather than smiling faces.

Occasionally, one member of a table of otherwise disinterested patrons will glance over in your direction and shout "Play some fucking Metallica" — or something equally poignant — before returning to his conversation without waiting for your response.

The physical location of the stage can have dire consequences on a bad night. If you are somewhat tucked away in the corner of the room, you can take the "background musician" route, disassociate yourself from the audience, and live to fight another day. But if the "stage" is set up near the flow of traffic, the gig becomes nightmarish as patrons walk past — directly in front of you — without any acknowledgment at all, ignoring your tip jar. You have literally become a living jukebox filled with pale imitations of the real thing, a non-feeling cyborg delivering music at the whim of others.

Sounds awesome, right?

Actually, this is dangerous territory. It can be deadly for a fragile psyche (a category that, tragically, is crowded with artistic types) particularly if multiple bad gigs run together. These are the nights that separate the wheat from the chaff, the stable personality from the slightly off, and reveal the answers to lingering, decade-old questions: Am I cut out for this? Do I really care? Is this the end game of all my work and effort?

You remind yourself that you're in good company. Every great musician has Bad Gig Stories, you point out, grasping at straws. The Beatles, Hendrix, Queen, Zamfir, Master of the Pan Flute; they all had to work through this. Every creative giant deals with failure and disappointment. Heck, some never experience success in their living years at all. During his life, Van Gogh was viewed as a crazy, talentless bum. Edgar Allen Poe died penniless in a ditch; Emily Dickinson, an eccentric old maid who rarely left her bedroom.

Even one of my modern-day heroes — Jim Croce — never got to really experience success. Although he was becoming known before perishing in a plane crash in 1973, the royalties had never caught up. He was just on the cusp of reaping some of the financial rewards of all those years of marginal gigs and embarrassing day jobs when the whole thing was snuffed out, just like that.

But you don't necessarily aspire to greatness or fame. You can't even imagine yourself as a rich and famous musician. You just want to survive with a little dignity, enjoy a modicum of acknowledgment for your craft, and make ends meet with a decent, paid-for vehicle and a good guitar.

It doesn't seem like too much to ask.

These are the bright, inspirational thoughts that run through your mind as you try desperately to run out the clock by playing the chord changes to "Hotel California" for 28 straight minutes. Next up will be McCartney's "Blackbird," and you'll run through that a solid three times without singing a note.

Mercifully, after several eons, after amoebas have evolved into giraffes and the Himalayas have eroded into a flat, sandy desert, the gig ends. I place my guitar into its soft-shell case, zip it up, wave goodnight to Rhonda, and head upstairs to my apartment.

At least I don't have to walk the plank, I remind myself as I toss a bag of popcorn into the tiny microwave.

15

CLOSE SHAVES

Christiansted was electric, crackling with anticipation.

Today was Ernest Alvarez's 50th birthday. Sure, that's a monumental number, but it held even more significance for Ernest. Tonight, in front of his many friends and acquaintances, he would shave off his famous beard.

Now, this is a big deal for anyone who has spent years cultivating a bushy face that was as impressive as Ernest's, but in his case, the stakes were drastically higher than an investment of time without a razor. Soggy Beard Adventures was arguably the most famous single business in Christiansted, so a substantial part of the town's identity was thanks to — and dependent upon — Ernest's massive whiskers. When tourists booked trips aboard the Cutlass, they expected to meet Soggy Beard himself as part of the package, and if this didn't happen, they were visibly disappointed.

Soggy Beard's beard was indubitably big business.

But tonight, the beard was coming off because, for more than a decade, Ernest had told people he would shave it when he turned 50. People remembered and were holding him to it.

"I guess I never thought 50 would arrive," he admitted to me later. "It snuck up on me."

The bottom line was, everyone wanted to see what Ernest looked like without what amounted to a full-grown sheepdog growing out of his lower face. People also wanted to be there in case something unexpected dropped out during the shaving, like a ferret or a beach chair or perhaps, a family of Vietnamese boat people who had taken a wrong turn.

My gig began as usual at 9 pm with the big event scheduled for 12 midnight. By 11:55, The Mizzenmast Bar was bursting at the seams with locals and whatever curious tourists managed to squeeze in. I vacated the stage so it could be set up for Ernest. A local husband/wife hairdressing team, Carlos and Marina, would do the shaving honors.

As the clocked ticked over to 12 am, Ernest appeared from the back hallway of The Mizzenmast already wearing a large barber apron around his neck and made a dramatic entrance to the stage to raucous cheers. After the big man settled into a makeshift barber chair on the stage, Carlos brandished an enormous pair of what appeared to be sheep shears, holding them over his head as the crowd erupted. He then looked at Ernest, back at the shears, and seemed to think of something else. Dropping the shears, he reached into a large bag and came out with an even larger set of hedge clippers.

More cheers.

But that wasn't good enough, so he dropped the clippers, disappeared around the corner, and leaped back onto the stage with a full-sized chain saw.

By now, The Mizzenmast was in danger of burning down.

The jokes completed, Marina made short work of the beard, trimming it off with a few passes of a set of clippers while Carlos blocked the view of Ernest from the audience. Marina then lathered him up and carefully shaved his face with a straight razor. When they finished, I made a dramatic announcement over the PA system, introducing the new-and-improved Ernest Alvarez as the big man jumped up and ripped the barber apron off to reveal that he was dressed in a dress shirt, tie, and slacks underneath.

The crowd gasped. The now clean-shaven Ernest looked exactly like Robin Williams and was unrecognizable as Ernest Alvarez.

There was a beat of stunned silence followed by a deafening exclamation.

All of this was, of course, nothing more than another excuse — albeit a good one — for the locals to get hammered. Any mundane thing could be twisted into a reason to drink on St. Croix.

Ernest shaves his beard? Fill 'em up!

The Bulls just won the NBA Championship? Pour me another! (Never mind the fact that Chicago is 2,500 miles away and nobody on St. Croix cares.)

Queen Cross Street gets repaved tomorrow? Skoal!

We snorkeled at Buck Island today and nobody died? Let's celebrate!

But fueled by the anticipation of the shaving event and the Big Reveal, this particular evening was lurching out of control and was in danger of flying off the rails. Rhonda and another bartender were dispensing alcohol as fast as they could shove bottles and glasses into the hands of patrons, and the venue was becoming a fire marshal's worst nightmare, with bodies spilling out onto the front patio and down the staircase. Long after Ernest had said his goodnights and escaped, the dance floor continued to fill as I played one crowd favorite after another.

I was not in fine form. I had let my hair down a little too much and was partaking of a continuous stream of tequila shots that were finding their way to the stage.

"Shot, shot, shot, shot...!" the crowd would chat in unison between tunes, encouraging me to down yet another glass.

On a typical night, I would've sipped two, perhaps three beers over the course of a four-hour gig, often finishing entirely sober. Tonight, though, was different. I was being counseled by the same stupid voice that had gotten me into trouble with the Jägermeister nearly two months earlier. I'm sure that my guitar playing and singing had become laughable, although to the equally inebriated ears throughout the room, I may have sounded great. Hard to say. But had I been able to listen to myself objectively, I would've no doubt been mortified. Within two decades, cell-phone video would alter the consequences of public foolishness forever, but in 1995, acting like an idiot was rarely recorded by anything more than someone's unreliable and, therefore, *debatable* memory.

Thank God.

As if the room needed any more reason to approach combustion, I poured nitroglycerine on the flames by launching into Buffett's most socially unacceptable song of all, the ultimate anthem to debauchery. You know the one. It has a whole lot to do with drinking and screwing, in that order.

Pandemonium. By the end of the first line, around 200 patrons (the room was approved for 75) had linked arms and were now swaying in time to my playing, overpowering the PA system by shouting Buffett's lyrics in a single monotone chant. During the instrumental section, the dance floor devolved into a near Roman orgy with couples making out, openly groping each other, and pouring shots of liquor down each other's gullets. More shot glasses and full bottles of beer were deposited on top of the amp beside my stool along with napkins containing song requests, $5 and $10 bills, and phone numbers. One girl approached the stage and, with her back to the crowd, pulled up her shirt and bra and flashed me with enormous brown breasts before cheering and dancing back into the throng.

The horizon tilted as Dr. Jekyll struggled to remain in control. Through my rapidly diminishing brain function, a single thought began tapping at the synapses that were struggling to fire:

Walk the plank... Walk the plank...

I began to see the audience as a boatload of pirates, each brandishing his sword and screaming at me to play "Blow the Man Down" over and over again.

I'm a deep water sailor just in from Hong Kong
To my way hey, blow the man down
If you'll give me some grog, I'll sing you a song
Give me some time to blow the man down

The room shifted slightly as the lyrics morphed and the faces began to swirl into indistinguishable shapes. The world was falling away and then returning with every heartbeat. My vision cleared, and I realized I was playing the song on autopilot. Other lyrics and chord changes, all from songs I'd written in the various apartments and hotel rooms over the past 10 years, began scrolling past my mind's eye like cards in a Rolodex, but my voice and hands were well-trained, locked onto the Buffett tune. I could hear myself playing from far away, a tinny voice on a transistor radio. But now, the song was "Blow the Man Down." The Mizzenmast faded to black as if someone was lowering a dimmer switch, and the music was faint, barely audible, then nothing.

Candles. The creaking of wood.

I was no longer in The Mizzenmast. The galley of a ship swayed gently from side to side, and the air was thick with the smoke of tobacco and hemp, and close with body odor. A humid sea breeze entering through open portholes stirred the air like stew in a cauldron, quivering the flames of the candles placed about the galley. I became aware that I was sawing at a fiddle, creating a choppy, squawking melody that I sang along with.

'Tis when a Black Baller is clear of the land
To me way hey, blow the man down
Our Boatswain then gives us the word of command

Give me some time to blow the man down

The lyrics were odd and unfamiliar, yet they rolled off my tongue easily.

Around the room were strewn heavily bearded men, some wearing tri-corn hats, each holding large tankards of liquid that sloshed onto the floor as they swayed in time with the song. They wore strange clothes — some with gaudy striped pants and sashes, others with bright red military jackets, stained and filthy. The candlelight glinted off of the metal of the swords, scabbards, and muskets hanging from their belts.

One pirate approached me, peering into my face, our noses nearly touching. He wore a huge, black beard that was festooned with multi-colored beads and ribbons. His drooping mustache was covered in white foam, no doubt collected from his tankard of ale.

"Play it ag'n, mate," he hissed. "Dunna stop 'til I say or ye'll be swimmin' wi' sharks."

(Sure, he sounded exactly like an animatronic villain from the "Pirates of the Caribbean" ride at Disney World, but that's what my 20th Century brain had to work with.)

I realized I had stopped sawing on the fiddle, and the room had gone quiet. As the boat swayed, various metallic objects hanging from the low ceiling clanked together.

"Sure, I'll play it again," I heard myself stammer. "I generally play for tips, though. Can you help a brother out?"

The pirate grasped my shoulder with a thick, hairy hand, each finger crowded with gold and silver rings.

"Aye, yer a cheeky one, ain't ye?" he said.

He glanced back at his fellow shipmates and grinned with brown teeth.

"He's a cheeky one!" he bellowed with a booming laugh, eliciting a chorus of guffaws from the others.

Someone pulled the dimmer switch down again and, once

more, the room went black. Then, another hand was on my shoulder, shaking.

"Hey, bro, you OK? Dude! You OK?"

A face came into focus. A young man wearing an orange University of Florida cap was standing before me. I became aware that although I still sat on my stool, I had stopped playing.

I had blacked out.

Dozens of eyes were on me, and the room had fallen mostly silent. I willed myself into consciousness.

"Back in 15!" I shouted into the microphone, slurring a little. "Sorry!"

After a couple of clumsy tries, I managed to flip the switch on the CD player connected to the PA and the opening chords of Paul Simon's "You Can Call Me Al" blasted through the room. Within seconds, the audience had forgotten about the embarrassing episode with the nameless guitar player and was dancing to thumping bass and African rhythm.

I lurched off the stage and through the crowd, pushing my way through the bodies until I reached the safety of the back hallway. Stumbling through the darkness to the exit, I walked out onto the open-air corridor of the defunct hotel, collapsing onto the top step of the staircase. My heart pounded.

I was mortified. I had breached my own cardinal rule of always showing up, being a professional, and giving my employer his or her money's worth. Sure, I had done some dumb things on stage before, but never had I lost consciousness. It was unforgivable.

The night was clear. Even through the ambient light of the town, the stars seemed close.

I stared at them, trying to align my thoughts and clear the blurriness. The episode on the stool had shocked me nearly into sobriety, but not quite. I was still unsteady, but my brain had once again become my own, although I wasn't sure this was a good thing.

What are you doing? What are you becoming?

Even in drunkenness, I found myself in the same place as that day in my Nashville apartment after Ernest had offered me the job, that uncomfortable spot where I forced myself to take stock. I didn't want to. I wanted to just move on, go have another drink, and take the girl who had shown me her boobs back to my room and engage in uninhibited hedonism. I wanted to go full-on Mr. Hyde.

This is the spice of life! I told myself. Make the most of it. This place, the drinks, the girls ... it's the cinnamon, the saffron, the turmeric, the curry!

But I knew the truth. I couldn't avoid it. These things may be exotic, but I was not.

I was salt.

16

ESCAPES

The following week — the last of my time on St. Croix — was different. Although I put everything I had into my performances, I knew that something was missing. It wasn't something that anyone else would probably notice, but I could feel it. There was a sense that I'd entered a new chapter, but I had no idea what it was titled and what it might hold for me.

My final night at The Mizzenmast, a Thursday, was a bit of a train wreck. Although I hadn't announced it publicly, word had leaked out that this was my swan song on the island, which worked both for and against me. On the positive side, nearly every acquaintance that I had made showed up. On the negative side, same thing.

To be more specific, there were simultaneously three women in the audience that I had... er... *befriended* over the past two weeks, and each was unaware of the existence of the other two. I inferred by their presentation and demeanor that each expected a final hurrah, as it were, which placed me in a decidedly delicate predicament.

This would require some fancy footwork.

My first plan was to wait them out. I would forgo my scheduled intermissions and hope that two of them would finally give up and leave, much like a treed mountain lion trying to outlast a pack of very sexy baying hounds, each of which who wants to make passionate love to the mountain lion.

OK, so that analogy doesn't work at all, but you see what I'm getting at.

My plan didn't work, either. All three women stubbornly sat there for four hours, smiling demurely and sending up obscene notes on napkins while I played until my voice had nearly given out, my fingers were beginning to cramp, and my bladder was in danger of exploding, which would've been an unseemly ending to my stay on St. Croix.

Also during this debacle, my buddy and fellow musician, Jim Brady, was playing his own gig at the open-air, rooftop restaurant in the building immediately next door to the Mizzenmast building. Both audiences and musicians could easily hear the other, which made for not only a terrible clash of rhythms, keys, and notes — imagine "Changes in Latitudes" and "Bad, Bad, Leroy Brown" being played over two different stereos at the same time in the same room — but also a fertile comic environment. Though we couldn't see each other, Jim and I mercilessly messed with one another through our respective PA systems. Both gigs dissolved into a barrage of raunchy jokes and probably unlistenable music.

But through it all, the three stubborn ladies — Angie, a jewelry store clerk; Stef, a newspaper writer; and Becky, a kindergarten teacher — stayed glued to their tables. Even worse, it appeared that over the course of the evening, they somehow became aware of each other and began shooting looks of death and homicide back and forth across the room, creating an unbearable tension that, if visible, would've resembled that laser obstacle course Tom Cruise had to contend with in *Mission Impossible*. Unfortunately for them and me, nobody would back down. I was trapped on the stage, hoping that the crowded, public venue would dissuade any of them from actually attacking me or each other.

I played dumb, appearing to be entirely invested in my performance. In desperation, I was hatching schemes on one side of my brain while singing and playing the guitar with the other. It felt like an episode of *Seinfeld*, but wasn't nearly as funny.

One plan involved me lighting a fire in the bathroom. In the panic that followed, I would blend into the escaping throngs and simply walk away. Hopefully, The Mizzenmast wouldn't burn down, and nobody would be trampled to death.

Another had me bribing the local police to come arrest me for possession of something and haul me off to the relative safety of the St. Croix jail, but I was afraid that more than one of the girls might show up and try to bail me out, thus creating even more chaos.

The simplest, most elegant plan was the one I went with. About 30 minutes before closing, I made an announcement that I required a quick bathroom break and would be right back. As I stepped off the stage, I made eye contact with Rhonda, motioning her to meet me at the end of the bar top.

"I'm not coming back!" I hissed into her ear. "Just tell people that I passed out again or was kidnapped or something!"

"OK, but you owe me, you bastard," she hissed back, clearly aware of my conundrum. "I've enjoyed watching this all unfold, but I'll let you off the hook, only because I hate bloodshed in my bar. Call me in the morning."

And just like that, my Caribbean performance career ended in a delicious, if uncomfortable illustration of poetic justice. I had spent the past 15 years trying to seduce women with my music, but here, I had done my job a little too well and was now forced to flee like a third-world dictator escaping a military coup.

I ducked into the back hallway, sprinted up the darkened stairs, through the office, and into my apartment, locking the doors and hiding in the blackness until I was sure the coast was clear. Tomorrow, I would fly out of St. Croix in disgrace. (Not really, but I would certainly be careful as I left the building.)

THE NEXT MORNING, I EXITED THE OLD HOTEL LIKE A soldier easing through a city infested with snipers. Although I was pretty sure the three women were all at their respective jobs, I was still nervous. Rhonda and her dilapidated Toyota pickup waited for me on the street. I carefully placed my suitcase and guitar onto the "safe" part of her truck bed and jumped into the passenger seat, glancing toward the adjacent rooftops.

"Drive, woman," I instructed, slipping down into the seat so I could monitor the rooftops. "Hellfire could rain down on me at any minute."

"You'd get no sympathy from me," she replied, pulling out onto the quiet street. "Remember, you get to go home today. I have to stay here and deal with whatever collateral damage you left behind. One of those crazy chicks might firebomb The Mizzenmast, for all I know."

We wound through the streets of Christiansted, ending up at a small cafe on the south side of town, a place known for its breakfast menu. When we walked in, I was shocked to find Frank Foley, Capt. Toussaint, and Woody seated at a long table.

"Well, I guess they'll let anybody in here," I said with a grin, shaking each hand. "This is a grand surprise."

Frank grunted and sipped a black coffee.

"I wouldn't get up at 10 am on my day off for just anybody," he said, peering over the rim of his square glasses. "Since you delivered on your promise of all those Buffett songs, I figured the least I could do is grace you with my presence."

"I'm honored, I guess."

"You should be. After that three-ring circus last night, you're lucky I'm not blackmailing your sorry ass for money. I would if I thought you had any."

The conversation continued like this, with wisecracks, ball-busting, and careful avoidance of anything resembling solemn goodbyes. Although I'd only known these folks for two months, the parties, music, shared isolation of sorts, and general absurdity of it all had created an odd sort of kinship. We knew that it was unlikely that we'd see each other again, but that we would live on in the stories we could now tell, destined to become even more absurd with the passing years.

Toussaint stood up abruptly as we were finishing our last bites of bacon and eggs.

"OK, I t'ink it's time for me to go and get somet'ing done," he said, peering down at me through his black shark eyes. "You were a good man to have around de boat. Take good care now."

He shook my hand and disappeared through the door without another word.

"Wow," said Rhonda. "That's the most I've heard him say in weeks. You must've made an impression."

My throat tightened suddenly, and I was caught off guard by a swell of emotion.

"It's mutual," I croaked. "That goes for all of y'all."

In the parking lot, I exchanged hearty handshakes with Frank and Woody, who were headed to Frank's house to watch St. Croix's own basketball legend, Tim Duncan, play a game for the San Antonio Spurs. I could hear them improvising a drinking game based on Duncan's projected rebound totals as they climbed into Frank's jeep.

Rhonda and I continued to the airport, retracing the route we had taken eight weeks ago. After retrieving my bags from her pickup, I gave Rhonda a tight embrace, and she kissed me lightly on the cheek. She stepped back and looked at me.

"You won't be back," she said with a bluntness typical of her New Englander heritage. "I can tell. Something changed you over the last few days."

I was stunned.

"Really?" I said. "You could tell?"

"Of course, I could tell. You look tired now. Not physically, but somewhere else. I may be young, but I've seen a lot in my years, and I can tell that you're not cut out for this madness. It's a shame for me because you're one of the best musicians we've ever had on the island, but you don't need this. I mean, how many more fucking times do you really want to play "Brown Eyed Girl" and "Margaritaville" anyway? Any jack-off can do that. You need to be doing your stuff, not somebody else's. Just my opinion, but I'm usually right."

I stared at the ground.

"Well, I don't know what to say to that," I replied. "Thanks for your confidence in me."

She climbed back into the Toyota and slammed the door shut, rust raining to the pavement underneath. Her brilliant grin shone through the open window as she backed out of the parking spot.

"Get on the fucking plane and don't crash," she said and drove away.

An hour later, the American Eagle prop plane took flight heading east and immediately turning north, flying over the island and town of Christiansted. In a window seat, I looked down over the buildings, picking out the tiny square that was the metal roof of my apartment atop The Mizzenmast.

"Farewell, palmetto bugs, you evil bastards," I said quietly. Retrieving a disposable camera from my backpack, I snapped a few photos as the shore met the ocean. These prints would be visited many times over the next 25 years, permanently stuck and yellowing behind the plastic of a cheap photo album.

As we climbed higher, I saw a tiny white dot in the waters

near Buck Island, a green circle ringed with a gradational swatch book of teal and blue. The dot was surely the Cutlass. Far below me, some tourist was trying in vain to adjust the strap of her rented swim goggles, excited to jump into the welcoming waters of the Caribbean and see her first parrotfish or school of blue tang.

The islands soon moved beyond my view and only blue water and sky filled the window. Exhaustion overtook me as I stared at the expanse, eyelids drooping. I pictured a tiny wooden ship, sails aloft, skidding those waves so many years ago. I could see the nameless young man, probably no more than just a boy, sawing his fiddle in the creaking galley as his drunken ship-mates called out requests. His repetition would've been far worse than mine, as there were only around 40 songs — or sea shanties — that would've been in the repertoire of a pirate's troubadour.

The young man takes a sip of ale, and plucks a string of his fiddle, tuning it slightly, as the older pirates shout out shanty titles.

"Leave her, Johnny!"

"All for me, grog!"

"Pump her dry!"

"Bonnie ship, the Diamond!"

"Blow the man down!"

"Keep yer fecking knickers on!" the troubadour shouts back at the unruly audience, eliciting a roar of laughter. "I'll play 'Blow the man down' again, but ye have to sing with! Otherwise, ye have nary nutmegs between ye, ye daft collection of Miss Mollys!"

I reclined my seat and closed my eyes, smiling.

You tell 'em, brother.

17

AM RADIO

One gig begets another. This was my mantra for years, and it was accurate. Having a two-month Caribbean house gig on my resume looked impressive, never mind the fact that I returned to Nashville with the grand total of $212 after repaying Ernest for fronting me half of my airfare.

Within a month of returning, though, I had booked another tropical house engagement, this time a three-month job on South Padre Island, Texas, at the Radisson Resort. Beginning around the first of June, I would do a 5-9 pm, Happy Hour gig on the Hammerhead Deck, I was told. I had no idea what that meant but couldn't have cared less. Those fools would be paying me $800 per week.

But before the gig began, I had two months of survival in Nashville. My roommate, John, and I traded occasional nights at a Holiday Inn gig that paid a whopping sum of $25 per night and worked temp jobs during the day. During one particularly fun stretch, I sold my old alto saxophone from the high school band for $400 to make rent. The same day, John managed to procure a roll of food stamps. Triumphantly, we strutted into the local Piggly Wiggly and dropped $50 worth of stamps on Lipton instant rice meals and canned chicken, enough to keep us going for another two weeks. It was a day that would rank high on the list of our greatest days ever. Two guaranteed weeks of shelter and sustenance constituted near royalty.

I was definitely back in Nashville.

During these months, I was also back to writing and recording demos, including several songs that would appear on my *Tallman* album two years later. After a demo was completed, the cassette tape seemed to disappear into a nondescript filing cabinet in my publisher's office, much like the Ark of the Covenant being wheeled into the giant warehouse at the end of *Raiders of the Lost Ark*. Reggie would give me a hard copy of a publishing contract to sign and return, along with one for me to keep, and the song I worked so hard on would fade into obscurity. To this day, these compositions lie forgotten and dormant, like one of those African fishes that burrow into the mud during the drought season and wait for the spring rains to return and bring them back to life.

The rain would never come.

What was I to do? There was nothing I *could* do but to write another song.

June arrived. The Radisson job was a sort of luxurious, spit-and-polished version of The Mizzenmast gig. Instead of a dank, palmetto bug-ridden apartment, they put me up in a 10th-floor, two-bedroom condo overlooking the ocean. If I'm being honest, it was ridiculous. I felt like a teenager who had broken into a luxury beach house and decided to live there for the summer, or until the cops or his parents came.

Financially, it was a windfall. I paid off credit cards, purchased new sound equipment, and even bought a Macintosh computer, though I had little idea of what to do with it, other than to join smutty online chat rooms and play computer golf via a CD ROM I had purchased from the mall in nearby McAllen, Texas. I was endlessly entertained by the strange sound of the dial-up modem making its mysterious connections, which apparently involved an electronic cello, a circus clown and several radios with very poor reception. It was hypnotic.

As part of my arrangement, I also received a 50-percent discount on food from the Radisson's restaurant. I'm sure they lost money on this deal, because nearly every night, I would finish my gig, put my PA system away, and walk straight into the dinner buffet. I theorized that if I approached the spread like a grizzly bear in the fall of the year, I could put on several layers of fat and survive the following six months in Nashville by simply hibernating, only waking to pee and to check messages on my answering machine. So I ate like a man possessed, shoveling in plate after plate of prime rib, baked potatoes, and enchiladas and refried beans on Mexican night.

It didn't work. I stubbornly maintained my 18-year-old metabolism. No matter how much I ate, the scale hovered at around 180 pounds.

Money and food notwithstanding, the gig was the same. Regardless of everything else I did, I once again became known as that guy who plays Buffett and Taylor.

During the early, daylight hours of the show, I often played parody songs for children who ran $5 bills up to the stage and deposited them shyly into my tip jar.

Later in the night, I moved into the predictable raucous numbers for the drinking, adult crowd, often including 30-something women who were letting their hair down on business trips far away from their husbands. I would later write a song called "Big Trouble in Paradise" as an homage to these lost ladies.

Now she's knocking down happy hour margaritas

Feeling like a natural-born senorita
Dancing like a fool to the Macarena
Nobody knows, nobody knows
She's feeling her control slipping through her fingers
Dancing with the band, singing with the singers
A Romeo casts a glance that lingers
Nobody knows

It was the same story, different location. I began to feel as if my life would forever exist on a shallow plane of meaningless physical encounters and the regurgitation of sing-along cover music. It's not that the South Padre audiences wouldn't have been receptive to original music; it's just that they were incapable of being receptive to it *there*. Listening to live music you've never heard before requires intentional, careful concentration and can only happen properly when everyone — both audience and performer — is on the same page and in the correct venue.

But in South Padre, much like St. Croix, the intention was to lose concentration, to edge toward inhibition. It was a no-win situation for playing original music.

For explicit, late-night rendezvous, however, the environment was productive. Instead of alcohol, weed, or the equally easy-to-acquire hard drugs, sins of the flesh was my addiction of choice. Unfortunately, though, and much like the character in "Big Trouble in Paradise," the negative consequences began to outweigh the short-term pleasures, a malady I couldn't have imagined 10 years earlier. By now, almost everyone I had grown up with was in loving, long-term relationships, many married with children. I found myself living vicariously through them instead of the other way around, and began to fall back to the nagging feeling I had cultivated on St. Croix:

Is this all there is?

~

BLOW THE MAN DOWN

ONE MONDAY MORNING, I RECEIVED A CALL FROM THE office of the Radisson's general manager, a guy named Martin, asking me to meet with him a few minutes later. When I walked into his office, Martin was seated with another fellow. They both stood up as I entered.

"Mark, this is Joe Leggett," said Martin. "Joe is a producer with the ABC television affiliate out of Houston, and he needs your help."

All I could think of was, *What the hell...?*

"What can I do for you?" I asked, shaking Joe's hand.

Joe was a short, slight man in his 40s, very professional and put together. He seemed weirdly happy, almost excited, to meet me. I was dressed in the usual — beer company t-shirt, cut-off jean shorts, flip-flops — and immediately felt under-dressed. But Joe didn't seem to notice or care.

"Mark, you don't know me, but I sure know you," he said, a massive grin on his face. "My daughter attends the University of Missouri, and I've seen you play at Widman's Bar in Columbia several times. We love your music and know your *Part of Me* CD up and down. I couldn't believe it when I saw your name on the marquee outside! I mean, what are the chances of that?"

"Wow! Oookay, so..."

"So, I'm producing the 'Miss Texas USA Pageant' for ABC this year, and we will be filming part of the show here at the Radisson," he continued without a pause. "I'd love to feature you in a segment with the girls. No big deal, just choose a song and play it for them on your regular stage. I think they would enjoy you and it would make for a cool addition to the show. Whaddya say?"

It was a bizarre moment. In a split second, I tried to process the fact that this guy had seen me play several times in a place many miles away, thought I was some kind of celebrity, and oh, by the way, was a television producer who wanted to place me amongst dozens of attractive women, the kind I used to daydream about alongside my Millennium Falcon model.

"Well...sure, I guess," I sputtered. "I mean, are you sure I'm the same Mark Johnson you're thinking of? I've done the math, and there are at least 700 Mark Johnsons in Texas alone."

Joe and Martin fell into hysterics over this while I looked around the room carefully for the camera I was sure was there. It had to be a prank.

But it wasn't. After knocking around a few ideas, we decided that I would play the Eagles' song, "Witchy Woman," for the girls. I wouldn't make any extra money for the performance but looked at it as a free demo for future gigs. (In retrospect, I definitely should've negotiated for some moolah.)

THE PAGEANT CONTESTANTS SHOWED UP THE following Thursday, and the Radisson became overrun with poofy blond hair. It was impressive, actually, as if South Padre Island had been transformed into what I always imagined Sweden to be.

That evening, a gaggle of television technicians descended on the Hammerhead Deck, wiring it for sound and placing cameras here and there. At around 7 pm, the contestants began flowing out of the restaurant and onto the deck until the entire place was full. I never found out for sure but estimated that there were at least 100 girls out there. Even though we were outside and a breeze was blowing in from the nearby Gulf of Mexico, the air became pungent with a combination of hair spray, Dentyne gum, and Tommy Girl perfume. It was intoxicating.

After the crew made a few adjustments to my sound and the cameras, I began playing "Witchy Woman." If I remember correctly, I did three takes.

The process was both exciting and weird, as if experiencing

an extremely realistic dream. This was the night that I discovered the power of the camera and fickleness of fame, real or perceived.

The director would give me the signal to begin, the cameras would light up, and off I went. As one, the contestants became enthralled with me, staring seductively as they mouthed the words of the song and swayed in place as if overtaken by my voice.

At first, I was nearly overwhelmed by the adulation. I mean, each one of these girls was clearly in love with me. Although I seemed to be 100-percent invested in the song, my fevered brain was actually thinking thoughts like:

- *Oh, yeah. I'm getting laid tonight, and*
- *A hundred hot-babe pageant girls think I'm famous right now. Do they know I didn't actually write this song? Should I tell them? and*
- *Oh, yeah. I'm getting laid tonight.*

But as soon as the take was over and the cameras stopped, the adulation ended as well. The contestants would chat with each other, reapply their lipstick, and redo their hair, often by flinging their heads violently forward and then back again. One hundred girls simultaneously tossing their heads back and forth created a strange, strobe-light effect and swishing noise, the combination of which made me a little nauseous. It was like being at a Twisted Sister concert with the sound turned off.

Most disconcerting of all, though, was how easily the girls switched between "I wanna have monkey sex with you right this minute, and I don't care who sees" and "When's the next fake event where I need to look interested for the camera?" It soon became apparent, even to a doofus like me, that the real motivation was camera time. The guy on the stage was simply a prop. I could've looked like Jabba The Hut, and it wouldn't have mattered.

But I dutifully pressed on.

Oooooo, oooooo, Witch-ay woh-man...

And then, we were done. In unison, the girls shouted, "Thank you!" and were herded back into the Radisson like a flowing blond river as the technicians disassembled the gear. Suddenly, I was alone again. I packed up my guitar and went to see what kind of Mexican food was on the buffet.

A week later, as the pageant was broadcast across Texas, I sat in my condo and watched myself sing a cover song to a bunch of girls who would never remember my name. Aside from a couple of Radisson staff members, the event was hardly mentioned again, and I went about my gig.

That summer provided me with two invaluable takeaways:

1. The pursuit of fame is a self-serving, often shallow endeavor that rarely delivers the desired result, and
2. I got to play "Witchy Woman" for 100 hot babes at the same time. Suck on that, Billy Dean!

RETURNING TO MUSIC CITY IN EARLY SEPTEMBER, I rented a $300-per-month attic apartment in what was reputed to be the oldest house in East Nashville. Having just spent three months in what was comparatively the Ritz, my living quarters took a little getting used to.

The apartment comprised a hallway, two bedrooms — one that was being used for storage — and a tiny bathroom. Neither bedroom had an HVAC vent. The only one of those was in the hall, so I devised a crude ductwork system composed of multiple cardboard boxes connected by packing tape and leading from the single vent in the hallway floor and through the open door of the bedroom. It worked fine if you didn't mind stepping over a tube of cardboard boxes a dozen times every day.

Showering was its own adventure. The plastic stall, you see, had been built into the house's slanting roofline such that I was required to either squat slightly during the showering process, or stand with my head cocked at an angle, like a confused puppy. The plumber (I'll bet as a practical joke) had also installed the showerhead facing the shower entrance. This meant that no matter how hard you tried to avoid it, you were blasted with cold water upon turning on the faucet.

Sometimes, the glamour of the professional music business is so palpable, it nearly makes you weep.

I returned to my routine of ridiculous daily temp jobs, occasional travel gigs, and songwriting. One day in autumn of that year, 1995, Reggie called me.

"This is cool," he said. "I got your Christmas song on this holiday season's CDX."

"Umm, speak English, please."

"Oh, sorry. CDX is the company that sends each month's single releases to country radio," Reggie explained. "It's what the DJs use to program their music. Every week, they send a compilation CD to every country music station in America. Yours will be on their special Christmas edition."

"But my song isn't on an album," I said, confused. "It's not signed to a label. How can it be released?"

"It can because I know the guy that runs CDX and he was short on new Christmas material," Reggie laughed. "This is good news. Sure, it probably won't make much money, but hell, somebody will play it!"

With that little tidbit, I celebrated by driving to the nearby Wendy's and splurging on an oversized chocolate chip cookie.

∼

3 PM, DECEMBER 24, 1995.

Two days earlier, the Family Truckster had managed to make the 400-mile journey across Tennessee, up into Virginia, and back across the border into North Carolina without exploding into a cloud of rusty 1978 molecules, like I fully expected it would. I was surprised when I pulled into my parents' driveway slightly ahead of schedule.

This afternoon, I was decorating our mountain home for the holidays alone because Mom, Dad, and my brother, Greg, were still in Raleigh, buttoning up the facilities on their various Christmas tree lots. My sister, Teri, who lived in Raleigh, would join them for the trip home.

It had become tradition — after nearly 30 years in the Christmas tree business — for my family to roll in on Christmas Eve, exhausted but happy. It was also customary for us to erect our own Christmas tree late on Dec. 24, often after midnight, much to Santa's dismay. My dad always said that the Johnsons were the last family in North Carolina to put up their tree, and he was probably right. Tonight, we would all gather, decorate the most perfect tree on the planet, and listen to the Danny Davis and the Nashville Brass Christmas album repeatedly over the old record player in the family room.

As I knew he would, Dad called me that afternoon and asked if I would go to one of our farms across the county and cut the tree he had tagged for the family. I grabbed one of his old chainsaws, a pair of work gloves and a heavy coat, and headed out onto the curvy mountain roads in the Truckster.

As I drove through the familiar rural landscape of my childhood, the year replayed itself in my mind. The Mizzenmast, the Cutlass, my feud with Fati Master, the blacking out incident on the barstool, the debauchery and fake fame of South Padre Island — it seemed impossible that these things had happened, and to me, no less. They had occurred but then vanished into the atmosphere, like your breath on a cold day, lingering just long enough to fix itself into your mind's eye.

Without thinking, I reached forward and switched on the Family Truckster's radio, which only worked on AM, and began flipping through the faint channels, hoping to catch Nat King Cole or Bing Crosby.

Suddenly, I passed a familiar note and voice, and it raised the hair on my neck and sent a spray of goose pimples across my arms. I turned the knob back until the frequency locked into the 17-year-old radio.

What the...?!

I recognized the voice because it was my own. It was my song, "My Family Christmas Tree."

I gasped and slammed on the brakes reflexively. The station wagon's back tires locked up with a squeal of rubber and fishtailed, leaving a curvy black streak down the road behind me. Like in a scene from *Starsky and Hutch*, the old Diplomat slid off the hardtop and into a gravel lot adjacent to Blevins Store, a small market and gas station. Gravel flew in all directions, and a cloud of gray dust drifted around and then past my car.

I was on the radio. Singing *my* song.

The signal began to fade as AM reception will do, so I threw the car in reverse and backed up until it improved, about 15 feet. It faded again, so I pulled forward another five feet. Now, back again, another 10 feet. To anyone watching, it probably looked like I was trying to kill a snake with the station wagon. But the channel, although faint, finally stabilized.

I couldn't believe my ears. That was my voice and, more importantly, those were my words being broadcast across airwaves, originating from a station somewhere distant and not owned and operated by any member of my immediate family. The over-the-top irony struck me like a sledgehammer: As I drove to harvest my family's Christmas tree — on Christmas

Eve, no doubt — I was hearing "My Family Christmas Tree" on the air for the first time.

And Lord, I pray that I might always find it standing tall
Surrounded by the people that I love most of all
May it grow just like a redwood and stay forever green
That's my family Christmas tree, that's my family Christmas tree

I could scarcely breathe. The bluegrass-influenced song about my yuletide heritage ended in a descending phrase featuring my acoustic guitar, Brent Rowan's shimmering mandolin, and Hubert "Hoot" Hester's fiddle. As it faded away, the DJ spoke.

"That's 'My Family Christmas Tree' by a brand-new artist, name of Mark Johnson," he said with a mountain accent. "Good stuff. We'll listen out for more by Mr. Johnson. And now, here's the latest from Aaron Tippin..."

I sat alone in the old station wagon, grinning through tears like a fool. A thumbtack plopped from the ceiling onto my lap and the headboard fabric drooped onto my head.

I would hear "My Family Christmas Tree" seven more times that evening — December 24, 1995 — on seven different AM stations.

EPILOGUE

Rhonda Shanks remained in St. Croix for only two more years. Soon after I left the island, she began dating an older man with whom she saw a real future, but was shocked when he was arrested at the airport in St. Thomas on drug smuggling charges. He was taken straight to a federal prison on the island and Rhonda never saw him again.

She returned to the states, eventually taking over a screw manufacturing business from her aging parents. Today, she is happily married and living a life of early and luxurious retirement in Florida, having sold the business.

Frank Foley continued to work on St. Croix for another 15 years, only leaving after the Hess Oil plant closed up shop in 2010. He moved to Houston where he finished out his career with Hess before retiring in 2017. Frank now splits his time between Florida and Texas and enjoys visiting his grandkids. Rumor has it that he still attends every Jimmy Buffett concert within a three-state radius.

Ernest Alvarez, a.k.a. "Soggy Beard," is now in his '70s and retired in 2016. He lives half his year in St. Croix and half in his home state of Oregon, but still owns an interest in Soggy Beard

Adventures and makes occasional surprise appearances on the dock before the persistent Cutlass shoves off to Buck Island. Although he is now battling Parkinson's disease, Ernest remains a legend in Christiansted, and every year dyes his now snowy white beard bright green for St. Patrick's Day.

Ernest sold The Mizzenmast only four months after I left. It continued to serve as a bar under other names for a decade but now sits vacant.

Rhonda told me that Capt. Toussaint died some years back but is unsure of when. She heard a rumor that he expired while in bed with two cuties on the island of Aruba.

My old roommate, John Foster, became a successful musician, an accomplished guitar player and singer touring with country artists Sammy Kershaw and Steve Holy, and even the Beach Boys. He now fronts Nashville's most popular Beatles and Fleetwood Mac tribute bands and remains in high demand as a session musician.

As for me, I never became a rich and famous singer/songwriter, as you have already surmised. "My Family Christmas Tree" charted on several independent music charts, but without label support, faded quickly.

In 1997, I released my final collection of original music, *Tallman*. It featured some of the best studio musicians in the business — including mandolin legend Sam Bush — and I had high hopes that it would get me signed to a major label, but that wasn't in the cards. I again found myself dealing with either confused or apathetic record executives who were much more interested in the next hunky "hat act" or formulaic pickup truck/small-town-water tank/tractor-driving/high-school-sweetheart song or singer.

I clearly didn't represent that genre and never would. I had done my best, but the indifferent industry response was a mortal blow that killed my internal drive to keep pushing and living a transient existence. After playing a summertime festival in my hometown of West Jefferson, North Carolina, in 1998, I decided my life as a full-time troubadour had run its course.

Some people might say I gave up.

I guess that's not totally untrue, although it does sound a little harsh. I like to think that I merely completed the musician phase of my life. It's easy to blame my lack of stardom on bad luck, improper advice, or other things beyond my control. The fact was, I would never be quite good enough as a performer to break through that mainstream "success" wall and I just didn't have the commitment to keep on fighting.

The good news, however, is that only a few months after the South Padre gig, my brother introduced me to a tall, beautiful brunette from Northern Virginia who had relocated to West Jefferson to run a small non-profit. Of everything that had occurred over the past few years, this was the most outrageous and unexpected — I fell head over heels in love.

Similar to landing major-label record deals, finding love was something that happened to other people, not me. Good things, I thought, were either fleeting or to be met with cynicism, like Charlie Brown's suspicion that Lucy would pull the football away at the last second. But in this case, I quickly went all in. Lucy finally held the ball in place, and I kicked it, a 75-yard field goal that sailed through the uprights.

Holly and I were married May 3, 1997, and I very selfishly moved her to Nashville. Between 2000 and 2007, we produced three children — Sam, Ava, and Pete — and the empty uncertainties of my careless youth began to fade. I became a person upon whom other humans depended and looked to for guidance. What a concept! I became a husband and a dad.

After hanging up the guitar in 1998, I found myself brimming with a confidence born of years of public performances, heartbreaking rejections, and soaring successes. Although I was unsure of where life would point me next, I felt intimidated by very few things (with the glaring exception of fatherhood). For more than a decade, I had thrown myself into one unknown and potentially perilous situation after another, showing up to places I'd never been, dealing with people I'd never met, and exposing myself to possible humiliation night after night. I was now protected by a nearly impenetrable emotional suit of armor that sent me strutting into job interviews with the cockiness of a Top Gun aviator.

Entirely unqualified on paper, I conned my way into a graphic design job at a small marketing agency in Nashville. My first day on the job, I was told to create a logo while the boss stood behind me and watched. I had never touched an IBM computer in my life (I was a Mac guy) nor opened the graphics program, CorelDraw, but had to act like I knew what I was doing. It was exactly like playing an unrehearsed cover tune on request before a live audience, making it up on the fly. Somehow, I passed the audition.

Within a year, I had launched my own home-based firm that persisted for an unlikely five years. I named the company "Gecko Graphics" in honor of my lizard friends on St. Croix. This led to a 10-year position as an editor for an agricultural magazine and later, several years as a communications director for a wildlife conservation non-profit.

I found that the process of composing hundreds of songs had instilled a sense of brevity in my long-form writing and had trained me to make every word count. The pressures of performance had made me undaunted by normally distressing things like copy deadlines. Time and again, my years as a musician and songwriter served me in unexpected and valuable ways.

In 2017, Holly and I founded the most improbable business of all — a trekking company providing epic adventures into the Nepali Himalayan Mountains. I published my first book, *Doofus Dad Does Everest Base Camp*, in November 2018, a memoir of our inaugural trek.

At first blush, these roads seem divergent and random, but

for me, they are tributaries that feed into a single river. As I stood at the foot of Mount Everest on April 7, 2018, I thought of that night in a North Carolina horse barn so long ago. My 13-year-old self was on the cusp of a journey that would take him far beyond his own expectations. The wish for adventure had come true, along with many more that I couldn't have imagined at that age.

And yet, those 13 years in music remain, for me, a singular experience.

To this day, recalling them is like watching a blurry, low-resolution YouTube video featuring someone else, a longhaired guy who kind of resembles me. I still have the occasional nightmare about performing for indifferent patrons with a faulty PA system and drooping microphone stand, and wake up in a sweaty panic. But I also have good dreams, long, luxuriant scenes of playing entire songs — actual chords, lyrics, and all — for adoring, applauding audiences. These dreams feel like tiny gifts from God, reminding me that my path had been the correct one, even without the tour buses and platinum records and *Saturday Night Live* performances.

And what of St. Croix?

I'm convinced that the direction of my life was shaped inexplicably by my two months there, on the stage of The Mizzenmast, and on the deck of the Cutlass. Even while hiking through the Himalayas at better than 16,000 feet, I can still place myself in the galley of an imaginary pirate vessel, singing the favorite sea shanties of my shipmates over and over again.

As I was a walking down Paradise Street
Way hey blow the man down
A pretty young damsel I chanced for to meet.
Give me some time to blow the man down!

THE END.

ACKNOWLEDGMENTS

I am forever indebted to the following people for their help with this book: John Macy, Robin Moray, Ed Smith, Shea and Stacy Mulcare, John Foster, Dennis Ritchie, Michael Robertson, Doug Wayne, Kathy Helmers, Walter Stanford, and all my classmates at Ashe Central High School who cheered for "Bye, Bye, Love."

Thanks to my kids — Sam, Ava, and Pete — who allowed me to squirrel myself away in my office for months on end when I should've been cooking dinner and playing ping-pong. I owe y'all.

Thanks most of all to my wife and partner in life, Holly, for her courage in allowing me to relive and expose the sordid details of my wicked past, and for her ongoing and relentless love in spite of it all.

∼

I also want to send thanks to my awesome Launch Team, who invested their own valuable time in making this book a success. Thanks go to John Pendzinski, Eddie Brawner, Mary Harbage,

Brenda Bass, Franklin Brown, Teri Johnson Pasley, Jossie Canario-Lange, Robert Tretsch, Melissa Church Lawton, Kimberly Friedrichs, Michael Patrick St. Clair, Russ Moore, Jeff Brown, Michael Strauss, and Greg Brooks.

ABOUT THE AUTHOR

You just read this book, so you know a helluva lot about me already. I currently live in Kingston Springs, Tennessee, with my wife, Holly, and kids, Ava and Pete. Our oldest son, Sam, is in college, so I can't claim that I live with him.

In addition to books, I also write a blog called "Doofus Dad." Find that at *www.doofusdad.com.*

FINAL THOUGHTS

If you enjoyed this book, *please* consider dropping me a review at Amazon, Barnes & Noble, Kobo, or any other available place. This will help the book's visibility and, hopefully, allow me to continue writing books and avoiding real jobs. Also, Holly and I are launching a new podcast in early 2020. Look for "The How in the World Podcast" wherever you get your podcasts.

ALSO BY MARK E. JOHNSON

Doofus Dad Does Everest Base Camp: One of Planet Earth's epic adventures told by a slightly-less-than-epic guy

"Mark Johnson has a magical way of picking you up from your comfy reading chair and dropping you off in the heart of the cold and at times unforgiving Himalayas. I read the whole book in just a few quick sittings and constantly found myself laughing, biting my nails, and undeniably identifying with every ridiculous thing Mark found himself doing on his journey. If you enjoy grand adventures and a fair share of "dad humor," add Mark's EBC chronicle to your bookshelf now." ~ Tim Moore, The Penny Hoarder